John Henry Newman, Frederick George Lee

Lyrics of Light and Life

Original Poems

John Henry Newman, Frederick George Lee

Lyrics of Light and Life
Original Poems

ISBN/EAN: 9783744714174

Printed in Europe, USA, Canada, Australia, Japan

Cover: Foto ©Thomas Meinert / pixelio.de

More available books at **www.hansebooks.com**

LYRICS OF LIGHT AND LIFE.

Lyrics of Light and Life:

LIV. Original Poems by

Dr. John H. Newman, William Alexander, Bp. of Derry, Christina G. Rossetti, Aubrey de Vere, J. C. Earle, W. Chatterton Dix, Rev. Gerard Moultrie, Rev. Henry Nutcombe Oxenham, Rev. R. H. Baynes, H. W. Mozley, Rev. A. M. Morgan, Rev. Edward Caswall, B. Montgomerie Ranking, Rev. R. S. Hawker, Rev. John Purchas, Rev. W. J. Blew, Rev. Dr. Monsell, Hedley Vicars, H. M. Stuart, D. Mackworth Dolben, &c. Edited by the Rev. Frederick George Lee, D.C.L.

ALDI DISCIP. ANGL

London : PICKERING & CO., 196, Piccadilly.

1878.

Forte ſcutum Salus Ducum.

Dedicated with Refpect and Regard to the Right
Honourable Thomas Fortefcue, Lord Clermont,

 FIDE ET  CONSTANTIA.

And to Louifa, Lady Clermont,
of Ravenfdale Park, in the County of Louth.

✠ *Beati*  *pacifici.*

PREFATORY NOTE.

 CANNOT fend forth this volume with-
out placing on record my great obliga-
tions, and heartieſt thanks, to all thoſe
whoſe valued and truly-prized contribu-
tions have made it what it is. This I now do.

Planned more than ten years ago, and put aſide
for ſome time by other and more preſſing duties,
it has been to me at once an agreeable relaxation
and a very great pleaſure, from time to time, to
ſecure from many friends and others the various
Chriſtian Lyrics which follow,—for which I here
expreſs my ſincere acknowledgments. I feel deeply
honoured by having been permitted to gather and
arrange such a poetical poſy ; and this from ſo many
who have won their laurels.

Two of the contributors, whoſe memories are
frequently before me, my old and dear friend the
Rev. John Purchas, and Mr. Mackworth Dolben,
of Finedon Hall,—a young writer of intenſe refinement, deep ſpirituality, and great promiſe, (who
met an untimely death,) have paſſed away from
ſight and ken.

The poems of theſe writers may be all the more
valued, therefore, becauſe with them the pen has been
laid down, the hand is cold, and the heart is ſtill.

I have only to add that no author is responsible for anything more than his own contribution.

F. G. L.

All Saints' Vicarage, Lambeth,
November 4, 1874.

NOTE TO THE SECOND EDITION.

IT is a source of satisfaction to me that a book which appealed neither to the ordinary multitude nor to commonplace tastes, has so soon reached a second edition. This, having been carefully revised, only differs from the first in that it contains eleven new poems. To the respective authors of these I tender my sincere acknowledgments.

Since its publication three more of the original contributors have passed onward to the life beyond the grave—Mr. Hawker, the Vicar of Morwenstow; Father Caswall, of the Birmingham Oratory, and Dr. Monsell. *Requiescant in pace.*

F. G. L.

Invention of the Holy Cross,
1878.

TABLE OF CONTENTS.

Contents.

Contents.

"An arid plain, with rocky mountains lit,
From time to time, with funfhine, frowning by ;—
Such was my path.   Alone and folitary
I took my way.   So lone it might have been
My laft dread journey into Death's dark vale ;
(For each one takes that journey all alone.)
Above, black clouds ; around, the wailing wind ;
While onward, o'er the level plains of fand,
No ftreak of filver heralded the Day.
Yet on the wind, when o'er me darkeft night,
There came glad words with mufic weird and faint,
LYRICS OF LIGHT AND LIFE,—angelic ftrains
Echoed from Home on Earth or Home above,
To fpeed a footfore Wanderer on his way."

"*The Sorrows of Sewallis.*"

Lyrics of Light and Life.

BELOW AND ABOVE.

DOWN below, the wild November whiſt-
ling
Through the beech's dome of burning
red,
And the Autumn ſprinkling penitential
Duſt and aſhes on the cheſtnut's head.

Down below, a pall of airy purple,
Darkly hanging from the mountain ſide,
And the ſunſet from his eyebrow ſtaring
O'er the long roll of the leaden tide.

Up above, the tree with leaf unfading
By the everlaſting river's brink,
And the ſea of glaſs, beyond the margin
Never yet the ſun was known to ſink.

B

Down below, the white wings of the fea-bird,
     Dafh'd acrofs the furrows dark with mould,
Flitting with the memories of our childhood
     Through the trees now waxen pale and old.

Down below, imaginations quivering
     Through our human fpirits like the wind,
Thoughts that tofs like leaves about the woodland,
     Hopes like fea-birds flafh'd acrofs the mind.

Up above, the hoft no man can number,
     In white robes, a palm in every hand ;
Each fome work fublime for ever working,
     In the fpacious tracts of that great land.

Up above, the thoughts that know not anguifh,
     Tender care, fweet love for us below,
Noble pity free from anxious terror,
     Larger love without a touch of woe.

Down below, a fad myfterious mufic,
 Wailing through the woods and on the fhore,
Burdened with a grand majeftic fecret
 That keeps fweeping from us evermore.

Up above, a mufic that entwineth,
 With eternal threads of golden found,
The great poem of this ftrange exiftence,
 All whofe wondrous meaning hath been found.

Down below, the Church to whofe poor window
 Glory by the autumnal trees is lent,
And a knot of worfhippers in mourning,
 Miffing fome one at the Sacrament.

Up above, the burft of Alleluia,
 And (without the facramental mift
Wrapt around us like a funlit halo)
 The great vifion of the Face of Chrift.

Down below, cold funlight on the tombftones,
  And the green wet turf with faded flowers;
Winter rofes, once like young hopes burning,
  Now beneath the ivy dripped with fhowers.

And the new-made grave within the churchyard,
  And the white cap on that young face pale,
And the watcher, ever as it dufketh,
  Rocking to and fro with that long wail.

Up above, a crowned and happy fpirit,
  Like an infant in the eternal years,
Who fhall grow in love and light for ever,
  Ordered in his place among his peers.

O the fobbing of the winds of Autumn,
  And the funfet ftreak of ftormy gold,
And the poor heart, thinking in the churchyard,
  " Night is coming and the grave is cold."

O the pale and plaſhed and ſodden roſes,
   And the deſolate heart that grave above,
And the white cap ſhaking as it darkens
   Round that ſhrine of memory and love.

O the reſt for ever, and the rapture,
   And the Hand that wipes the tears away;
And the golden homes beyond the ſunſet,
   And the hope that watches o'er the clay!

WILLIAM ALEXANDER,
Biſhop of Derry.

All Saints' Day, 1857.

MY BIRTHDAY.

ET the fun fummon all his beams to hold
   Bright pageant in his court, the cloud-
    paved fky;
Earth trim her fields and leaf her copfes cold;
  Till the dull month with fummer-fplendour vie.
  It is my Birthday;—and I fain would try,
Albeit in rude, in heartfelt ftrains to praife
  My God, for He hath fhielded wondroufly
From harm and envious error all my ways,
And purged my mifty fight, and fixed on heaven
   my gaze.

Not in that mood, in which the infenfate crowd
  Of wealthy folly hail their natal day,—
With riot throng, and feaft, and greetings loud,
  Chafing all thoughts of God and heaven away.

Poor insect ! feebly daring, madly gay,
What ! joy becaufe the fulnefs of the year
   Marks thee for greedy death a riper prey ?
Is not the filence of the grave too near ?
Vieweft thou the end with glee, meet fcene for
     harrowing fear ?

Go then, infatuate ! where the feftive hall,
   The curious board, the oblivious wine invite ;
Speed with obfequious hafte at Pleafure's call,
   And with thy revels fcare the far-fpent night.
   Joy thee, that clearer dawn upon thy fight
The gates of death ;—and pride thee in thy fum
   Of guilty years, and thy increafing white
Of locks ; in age untimely frolickfome,
Make much of thy brief fpan, few years are yet to
     come !

Yet wifer fuch, than he whom blank defpair
   And foftered grief's ungainful toil enflave ;

Lodged in whofe furrowed brow thrives fretful care,
    Sour graft of blighted hope; who, when the
        wave
Of evil rufhes, yields,—yet claims to rave
At his own deed, as the ftern will of heaven.
    In footh againft his Maker idly brave,
Whom e'en the creature-world has toffed and driven,
Curfing the life he mars, " a boon fo kindly given."[1]

He dreams of mifchief; and that brainborn ill
    Man's open face bears in his jealous view.
Fain would he fly his doom; that doom is ftill
    His own black thoughts, and they muft aye
        purfue.
    Too proud for merriment, or the pure dew
Soft gliftening on the fympathizing cheek;
    As fome dark, lonely, evil-natured yew,

---

[1] " Is life a boon fo kindly given?" &c. — Vide *Childe Harold,* cant. ii.

Whofe poifonous fruit—fo fabling poets fpeak—
Beneath the moon's pale gleam the midnight hag
  doth feek.

No! give to me, Great Lord, the conftant foul,
 Nor fooled by pleafure nor enflaved by care;
Each rebel-paffion (for Thou canft) controul,
 And make me know the tempter's every fnare.
 What, though alone my fober hours I wear,
No friend in view, and fadnefs o'er my mind
 Throws her dark veil?—Thou but accord this
  prayer,
And I will blefs Thee for my birth, and find
That ftillnefs breathes fweet tones, and lonelinefs
  is kind.

Each coming year, O grant it to refine
 All purer motions of this anxious breaft;
Kindle the fteadfaft flame of love divine,
 And comfort me with holier thoughts poffeft;

Till this worn body flowly fink to reft,
This feeble fpirit to the fky afpire,—
  As fome long-prifon'd **dove** toward her neft—
There **to receive the gracious** full-toned lyre,
Bowed low before the **Throne 'mid** the bright feraph
  choir.

J. H. Newman.

Trinity College, Oxford.
February **21, 1819.**

A ROSE PLANT IN JERICHO.

T morn I plucked a rofe and gave it Thee,
 A rofe of joy and happy love and peace,
  A rofe with fcarce a thorn :
 But in the chillnefs of a fecond morn
My rofe-bufh drooped, and all its gay increafe
Was but one thorn that wounded me.

I plucked the thorn and offered it to Thee ;
 And for my thorn Thou gaveft love and peace,
  Not joy this mortal morn :
 If Thou haft given much treafure for a thorn,
 Wilt Thou not give me for my rofe increafe
Of gladnefs, and all fweets to me ?

My thorny rofe, my love and pain, to Thee
 I offer ; and I fet my heart in peace,

And rest upon my thorn :
  For verily I think to-morrow morn
  Shall bring me Paradise, my gift's increase,
Yea, give Thy very Self to me.

CHRISTINA G. ROSSETTI.

THE SILVER ARMY.

*"There is neither fpeech nor language : but their voices
are heard among them."*

I.

UTHLESSLY the bare bright wheel of
    antique Time goes round,
    And Middle Age has fet his foot on Youth's
    enchanted ground ;
The port has waxed more ftately, the brow has
    fterner grown,
The fmile is touched with fadnefs, and the man
    feels more alone.

II.

Ah, me ! the golden lovelocks are changing into
    grey,
For God's filver filent army, no man may keep at
    bay :

And since I may not frown you down, nor motion
    you away—
O silver, silent monitors! what is it ye would
    say ?

III.

" Where is 'the purple light of love,' and where
    the creeds of youth ?
The faith in Manhood's honour, the repose on
    Woman's truth ?
The summer friendship vanished when the storm
    began to rave,
And false Egeria slumbers calmly in her village
    grave.

IV.

" Life's gambler! thou hast lost thy stake—and
    what is left but gloom ?
The fairy palace of Romance transformed into a
    tomb.

Dry is now thy fountain, Numa !—gone the dreamy
    grotto life—
Where the glamour of the Nymph-land—lo ! the
    cold decorous wife ! ”

v.

O filver filent multitude ! Thefe voices are not
    thine,
Thy glittering mail was forgëd by a Hand that is
    Divine :
Numa has ftill a tryfting-place, Life's glory has not
    flown,
For holy wedlock's crownëd Queen reigns on
    Egeria's throne.

vi.

Still in my creed man's honour and woman's love
    abide—
The phantafy of Boyhood with that village maiden
    died.

The deep ſtrong heart of manhood, the worſhip of
  a life—
The ſtainleſs fame, the honoured name, theſe, theſe
  I gave my wife !

VII.

The chivalry of labour is toil for others done—
By the worker, not the dreamer, are the ſtar and
  mantle won ;
Who works for home and country, for him God's
  angel ſings—
"O labourer worthy of thy hire—the aureole and
  the wings."

VIII.

O mother of my children, the ſilvery hoſts of
  God
Bear in their hands enchanters' wands, and not th'
  avenging rod :

They point unto the land youth deemed fo very far
    away[1]—

But Heaven looks nearer to us when the hair is
    growing grey.

JOHN PURCHAS.

[1] " They fhall behold the land that is very far off."— *Ifaiah* xxxiij. 17.

THE BASILICA OF ST. MARK, VENICE.

STATELY palace of the Triune God,
A myſtic ſanctuary of gloom and gleam,
With marbled ſaints, where twinkling
lamps are hung,
And joyful bells ring out with ſilvery tongue,
Telling how ſwiftly moves on old Time's ſtream,
And how great races knew th' avenging rod.
Nor Occidental rites are here alone,
Nor Oriental forms.   Majeſtic ſongs
Of Mary, round Incarnate God's high Throne,
Sung by Her children, gathered nigh in throngs
Where ſtill repoſe the relics of Saint Mark.
Link of the Eaſt and Weſt, but One true Ark.

Nations ! turn eaſtward in thy weſtern pride,
Eaſterns look weſtward—Adria is bright !

Blue waters fleep around, or, night-ftarred, glide
  ·Near fhrines, 'mid Earth's dark defert, of God's
      Light.

In peace, Lord, may thy fervant now depart,
  My wondering eyes have feen this heavenly fight,
And I would choofe henceforth the better part :
  Grant it, O Chrift, whene'er draws on the Night,
  After Earth's toil and moil, to where is light,
Lord, may thy fervant then in peace depart !

FREDERICK GEORGE LEE.

Venice, *Nov.* 15, 1877.

A MAY CAROL.

IS this, indeed, our ancient earth ?
　　Or have we died in ſleep and riſen ?
　Has Earth, likė man, her ſecond birth ?
Riſes the palace from the priſon ?

Hills beyond hills aſcend the ſkies ;
　In winding valleys, heaven-ſuſpended,
Huge foreſts, rich as ſunſet's dyes,
　With rainbow-braided clouds are blended.

From melting ſnows through coverts dank
　White torrents ruſh to yon blue mere,
Flooding its glazed and graſſy bank,
　The mirror of the milk-white ſteer.

What means it ? Glory, fweetnefs, might ?
  Not thefe, but fomething holier far—
Shadows of Him that Light of Light,
  Whofe prieftly veftment all things are.

The veil of fenfe tranfparent grows :
  God's Face fhines out, that veil behind,
Like yonder fea-reflected fnows—
  Here man muft worfhip, or be blind.

AUBREY DE VERE.

FROM THE CLOISTER.

A FRAGMENT.

[*The monk* JEROME *ſeated in the cloiſter.*]

TO have wandered in the days that were,
Through the ſweet groves of green
     Academé !
Or ſhrouded in the night of olive boughs,
Have watched the ſtarry cluſters overhead
Twinkle and quiver in the perfumed breeze—
That breeze which, ſoftly wafted from afar,
Mingled with ruſtling leaves and fountain's ſplaſh,
The boyiſh laughter and the maiden's ſong.
Or couched among the beds of pale-pink thyme
That fringe Cephiſſus with his purple pools,
Have idly liſtened while ſweet voices ſung
Of all thoſe ancient victories of love
That never weary, and that never die.

Of Sappho's leap, Leander's nightly ſwim,
Of wandering Echo, and the Trojan maid,
For whom all ages ſhed their pitying tears :
Or that fair legend, deareſt of them all,
That tells us how the hyacinth was born.
Next to have mingled in the eager crowd
That, queſtioning, circled ſome philoſopher :
Young eyes that gliſtened, and young cheeks that
　　　glowed
For love of Truth, the great Indefinite.
Truth—beautiful as ſeem the diſtant hills,
Veiled in ſoft purple-crags, whereon is found
No tender plant in the uncreviced rock,
But clinging lichen, and black ſhrivelled moſs.—
So ſhould day paſs, till from the ſummer ſky,
Behind the marble ſhrines and palaces,
The big ſun ſank, reddening the Ægean Sea.
So ſhould life paſs, as flows the clear brown ſtream,
And ſcarcely ſtirs the water-lilies' leaves.
Life here, methinks, is like to ſome canal,

Dull, meafured, muddy, wafhing flowerlefs banks.
O funny Athens! home of life and love!
Free, joyous life that I may never live!
Warm, glowing love, that I may never know.
Home of Apollo, god of Poetry!
Dear bright-haired god, in whom I half believe,
Come to me, as thou didft come to Semele,
Trailing acrofs the hills thy faffron robe,
And catch me heavenward wrapped in golden mifts.

I weary of this fqualid holinefs;
I weary of thefe hot black draperies;
I weary of the incenfe-thickened air,
The chiming of the inevitable bells;
The chanting too!—can man be made for this—
To hold his tongue all day, and fing all night?

My boyhood, hurried over, but once gone
For ever mourned—return for one fhort hour!
Friends of paft days, light up thefe cloifter walls

With your bright prefences, and ftarry eyes,
And make the cold grey vaulting ring again
With tinkling laughter — Ah, they come! they
    come!
I fhut my eyes, and fancy that I hear
The funlit ripples kifs the willow boughs.

But I forget myfelf; I muft confefs
All this to-morrow : thoughts—oh, let me fee!—
Of difcontent, and floth, and a diflike
To hear the clanging of the blefled bells ;
And fomething elfe. Ah, well! all lovely things
That this vile earth affords—wood, mountain,
    ftream,
The regal faces, and the godlike eyes
We fee, the tender voices that we hear,
Are but mere fhadows : the reality
Is—what? A fomething up above the clouds.
From every carven niche the ftony faints
Stretch out their wafted hands in mute reproach ;

And from the Crucifix, the great wan Chriſt
Shows me His bleeding wounds and thorny crown.
Then, hark ! I hear from many a lonely grave,
From blood-ſtained ſands of amphitheatres,
From loathſome dungeon, and from blackened ſtake,
A cry—the martyrs' cry—" Behold the Man !"

I hate myſelf, I hate this myſtery,—
The dread neceſſity of ſuffering.
Is there no place in all the univerſe
To hide me in ? no little iſland girt
With waves to drown the echo of that cry,
" Behold the Man, the Man of Calvary " ?

[BROTHER FRANCIS *croſſing the cloiſter, ſings.*]
  Sweeteſt Jeſu, Thou art He
    To Whom my ſoul aſpires ;
  Sweeteſt Jeſu, Thou art He
    Whom my whole heart deſires.

To love Thee, oh the extaſy,
　The rapture and the joy !
All earthly loves ſoon paſs away,
　All earthly pleaſures cloy.

But whoſo loves the Son of God
　Of love ſhall never tire,
But through and through ſhall burn and glow
　With Love's undying fire.

　　　　　　　　　[*He enters the chapel.*]

DIGBY MACKWORTH DOLBEN.

DESECRATION.

 HOUSE of prayer once confecrate
To God's high fervice—defolate !
A ruin where once ftood a fhrine,
Bright with the Prefence all divine !
Tread foftly here ! 'tis hallowed ground,
And faithful hearts ftill find around
Traces of things which once were here
In days of love and reverent fear.

This is no common fpot of earth,
No place for idle words or mirth ;
Here ftreamed the taper's myftic light,
Here flafhed the waving cenfers bright,
Awhile the Church's ancient fong
Lingered thefe ftately aifles among,
And high myfterious words were faid
Which brought to men the Living Bread.

O fhame on thofe who will not own
The ruined fhrine God's altar throne !
What though long years have come and gone
Since the laft rite was duly done,
Since the laft Sacrament was given,
Since the laft prayer went up to Heaven !
True, men have wrought its fad difgrace,
But ftill it is God's Holy Place.

O it is eafy work to fay
" A purer Faith, a Gofpel day,
Put all fuch holy ground afide,
And count all Nature fanctified."
It is not hard to dogmatize
And preach of " fuperftitious lies ;"
To mock at " prieftcraft," and to fearch
For fome pet text to curfe the Church :

But it *is* hard to bear the jeer,
To have the World's cold-hearted fneer,

The sneer the World for ever flings
At holy men and sacred things.
Courage! who fight the Cross beneath
Must fight unto the very death!
Faith, Hope, and Love the World shall win
From self, from sacrilege and sin!

W. CHATTERTON DIX.

ON THE BAPTISM OF A CHILD.

MORNING.

BABE, awake! the fun is high,
See, its beams are in the fky;
Warm it fhines 'mid cloudlet torn,
On thy bright baptifmal morn.

Wake thee! for the Church to-day
Yearns to greet thee on thy way;
Hark! the bells ring joyfully,
Holy welcome, babe, for thee.

Child of Adam! doft thou bear
Stain of fin on face fo fair?
Gift of God, oh! muft we fee
Sin's dark heritage in thee?

Wake thee from thy light repoſe!
Holy Church would thee encloſe,
Thee within her arms would hold,
Make thee lamb of Jeſu's fold.

EVENING.

BABY ſleep! the ſun is low,
  Evening ſhadows come and go;
Sleep, for on thy gentle brow
Gleams the Croſs of Jeſus now.

Calm thou lieſt in thy cot,
All thy baby woes forgot;
Fair thy dreſs, thy face how fair,
God's own image thou doſt bear.

In the ftill baptifmal hour,
O'er thee fell the Spirit's power;
In the bleft Thrice-Holy Name,
Thou art wafhed from fin and fhame.

.

Brighteft drops of heavenly dew,
Then refrefhed thy foul anew;
Child of God thou art become,
Heir of His eternal Home.

'Neath the Crofs His children fight,
Boldly they maintain the right;
Thou His banner muft uphold,
And in His dear caufe be bold.

Sleep thee, babe, beneath His care,
Angels to thy cot repair;
Holy Guardians of the night
Guide thy tender dreams aright.

We around will kneel and pray
That the bleſſings wrought this day,
May through life ſuſtain thy ſoul
Till it reach the heavenly goal.

NORA BATT.

THE DEATH OF ERMENGARDE.

A FRAGMENT.

(A girl ſpeaks.)

SAD, ſweet end——
She ſat upon the threſhold of her door :
A long night's pain had left her living ſtill :
Her cheek was white ; but trembling round her lips,
And dimly o'er her face diffuſed, there lay
Something that, held in check by feebleneſs,
Yet tended to a ſmile.   A cloak, tight-drawn,
From the cold March-wind ſcreened her, ſave one
    hand
Stretched on her knee, that reached to where a beam,
Thin ſlip of watery ſunſhine, ſunſet's laſt,
Slanted through froſty branches.   On that beam
(It brightened well that faded hand), methought,
Reſted her eyes, half-cloſed.   It was not ſo :

For when I knelt and kiſſed that hand ill-warmed,
Smiling, ſhe ſaid, "The ſmall unwedded maid
Has miſſed her mark! You ſhould have kiſſed the
    ring!
Full fifty years upon a widowed hand
It holds its own. It takes its lateſt ſunſhine!"
She lived through all that night, and died while
    dawned
Through ſnows Saint Joſeph's morn.

AUBREY DE VERE.

INDIA'S DREAM.

INDUS.

BROTHER ! after fet of day
'Neath your weftern ftars I lay,
And I looked on other bowers,
And I dreamed of dreaming flowers.
O how fair the garden-glades !
O how ftrange their central fhades !
In the heart of leaf and bloom,
Lo ! a folitary tomb.

ANGLUS.

I too fee, but not in dream,
'Neath all ftars a garden gleam ;
All things fragrant, all things white,
There lie buried in the night.

Wonder not that one fhould die,
One in garden-tomb fhould lie,
When thou mayft that garden fcan
Made a tomb, the foul of man.

INDUS.

This life's captives break their chain,
And to funlight pafs again,
This life's captives hope—the grave,
Never has fet free its flave.
O the vifion of my head !
Empty was that garden-bed,
And a voice ftruck on my ear,
"He is rifen ! He is not here !"

ANGLUS.

I, not lefs, the winter flown,
See a vifion like thy own,
When, from a dead life unfeen,
Wave the fields with living green ;

I fhall fee, and thou, and all,
At the World's great funeral,
A true garden every tomb,
Whence the dead fhall fpring and bloom.

INDUS.

In the place where flowers blow
Gardeners pafs to and fro ;
One feemed fet to drefs and keep
The fair garden of my fleep.
O with wounded feet and hands
In the funrife here He ftands,
And I own Him, Seed, Sun, Showers,
Gardener of all God's flowers !

In the drought men water bring
Thirfty flowers watering :
I am thirfty ; flood thou me
With the Chrift of Calvary.

ANGLUS.

In the Name of Father, Son,
And of Him, the Holy One,
Live—and light the ſtarleſs ſod ;
England owes to Ind her God.

A. MIDDLEMORE MORGAN.

OUR REST.

IGHT falls apace, the fhades grow long
　　Athwart the dewy lawn ;
Blithe birds pipe out their evenfong,
　　Flowers clofe till welcome dawn.

Behind the hill-tops, finking low,
　　Paffed the great Sun away ;
Now paler fpreads fair faffron glow
　　Amid the deepening grey.

All feek repofe when night is nigh—
　　The tender doves their neft,
The lambs, fafe-folded, fleeping lie,
　　The babe on mother's breaft.

So ſeek we, Lord, in Thee to reſt,
　Who lengtheneſt out our days,
Meet offerings bring—of prayer our beſt,
　And ſweeteſt ſongs of praiſe.

Care fills our lives—our cares on Thee
　We caſt from day to day :
Thy Voice ſounds gently " Come to Me
　Who bare your ſins away."

Weak are our footſteps—Thine the power
　To raiſe us when we fall ;
Full oft we ſtray in evil hour,
　Do Thou our ſouls recall !

What if we loſe Thee ? whence our hope ?
　Who elſe can ſave or cheer ?
Dread were our doom unhelped to grope
　In blank deſpair and fear.

But Thou art ours—True ſtrength and ſtay ;
　　At morn our Bread of Life ;
Until the cloſing of Life's day
　　Our Peace 'mid toil and ſtrife.

Be with us, Jeſus, at the end,
　　When death-ſhades round us cloſe,
Light in our gloom in pity ſend,
　　And grant a ſweet repoſe.

E. Louisa Lee.

THE SISTER OF MERCY.

I.

SHE was his playmate when a child: and,
in Life's golden hours,
He loved her as he loved the ftars, as he
loved the ftarry flowers;
With crown of flowers he dowered her, and all the
wealth of May,
And fhe was his dream-angel by night and his fairy-
queen by day.

All day fhe was his fairy-queen, her realms of fairy
light
Were the wild woods beautiful with flowers, and
the fun-kiffed mountain height,

And the heather on the upland, and the fhingle by
the fea,
And wherever fhe went was fairy - land, and her
own true knight was he.

All night fhe was his dream-angel; no crown of
flowers was there,
But a crown of ftarry glory beamed around her
golden hair,
And not the funny fmile of day beneath that crofs
of light,
But a dreamy ftarry fmile, like the fmile of dewy
Night.

And often when in boyifh glee he prattled faft and
wild,
A ftrange, weird awe would mingle with his love
for that fair child;

And he ceased his childish talk, and a shadow on
    him lay,
For she seemed as though she heard him not, and
    her heart was far away.

He saw her once at eventide: the glorious sun
    went down,
And kissed her golden tresses as with an angel's
    crown,
And it lay upon her pale white face, and radiant
    brow upraised,
And he saw his own dream-angel, and trembled as
    he gazed.

He knew his own dream-angel: those eyes of
    heavenly love,
That dreamy starry smile beneath the kindling skies
    above;

And it burft upon his heart, like a flafh of awful
 light,
And fhe was his fairy-queen no more but his dream-
 angel of Night.

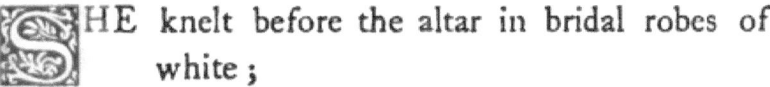

II.

SHE knelt before the altar in bridal robes of
 white ;
The church was beautiful with flowers, and blazed
 with ftarry light ;
There were flowers above the altar, and flowers
 wreathed in her hair,
And angels gazed upon her brow, and faw a ftar-
 crown there.

She knelt before the altar : the organ pealed on
 high,
They fwelled the wedding hymn of joy up to the
 liftening fky,

And angels' harps caught up the strain, and pealed
  it far away,
For God Himself comes down to claim a fair young
  bride to-day.

He saw his own dream-angel: the glorious sunlight
  came,
And kissed her virgin forehead with a crown of
  gold and flame;
And it lay upon her snowy flowers and on her
  golden hair,
But he was kneeling far away in sorrow and
  despair.

Strange strength arose within his soul: he let no
  teardrop start,
He checked each wild rebellious sob that trembled
  at his heart;

And he faid : " O God, I loved her more than all
the world befide,
But now Thy Will, Thy Will be done : I covet
not Thy Bride.

" I was not worthy of her love, this finful heart of
mine,
Of that pure virgin heart of hers, where every throb
was Thine ;
I was not worthy of her love ; and give her up to
Thee,
And Thou wilt hear her, if perchance fhe pray one
prayer for me."

The laft fweet hymn has died away : the awful rite
is o'er,
And fhe is now a Bride of Chrift, His love for
evermore :

And he bore his sorrow meekly, but his life had lost
    its light,
And she was his fairy-queen no more, but his dream-
    angel of night.

III.

HE lay upon the battle-field . . . . with faint
    and gasping breath,
Among the dying and the dead, on that grim field
    of death :
And no sweet hymn went up to God to soothe his
    aching head,
But the moaning of the dying and the wailing for
    the dead.

He lay upon the battle-field, and on his fevered
    brain,
A thousand memories of the past came rushing back
    again ;

His father and his mother, and the cottage by the
    lea,
And the chair where firſt he ſaid his prayers beſide
    his mother's knee :

And then his mother ſmiled on him, and tears were
    in his eye,
But he knew not why he wept for her, nor what it
    was to die ;
And the dance of his young life went on with all its
    joy and pain,
But he never ſaw his mother's ſmile, nor felt her
    kiſs again.

The wild woods and the leaping brooks, and a little
    child at play,
A little blue-eyed, fair-haired child, with a crown of
    early May ;

And her crown became a crown of ſtars, and her
    ſtar-croſſed brow grew bright,
And ſhe ſmiled a dreamy ſtarry ſmile, like the ſmile
    of dewy night.

An altar bright with lights and flowers, and a fair
    girl kneeling there,
And a breaking heart, and a ſtifled moan, and a
    faintly-whiſpered prayer,
And the moaning of the dying and the wailing for
    the dead,
And his own dream-angel's gentle arm around his
    drooping head.

He ſtarted from his reverie, and kneeling by his
    ſide
He ſaw his own dream-angel, and ſo in peace he
    died ;

While her prayers for him went up to God beneath
    the ftars all night,
And the Heavenly Bridegroom heard His Bride . . .
    and now he fleeps in light.

FOLLIOTT S. PIERPOINT.

THE OTHER SIDE.

" And when the even was come, he faid unto them, Let us pafs over unto the other fide."—St. Mark iv. 35.

THE day was done : befide the fultry fhore
    The cooling fhadows kiffed the reftlefs
    fea,
The words of wondrous wifdom now were o'er
    That make thy waves fo facred, Galilee !

The thronging multitude from far and nigh
    In eager hafte around His barque had preffed,
And, as He fpake, the hours paffed ftealthy by,
    And many a weary heart found peace and reft.

And then, as gently fell the evening dew,
    And the long day, with all its toil, was o'er,
The Mafter faith unto His chofen few,
    " Let us pafs over to the further fhore."

So, when our day is ended, and we ſtand
　　At even by the marge of Jordan's tide,
O may we firmly graſp His piercèd Hand,
　　And paſs triumphant to the " other ſide."

　　　　　　　ROBERT H. BAYNES.

WHITE IS THE COLOUR OF ANGELS.

" All glorious hues are in the pure white beam."
KEBLE.

WHITE is the colour of angels
　　And of innocent virgin fouls;
White is the orbèd night-queen
　　In the purple fky that rolls.

White is the hue of gladnefs,
　　And of hearts that know not grief;
White is the hue that Sadnefs
　　Aye looks to for relief.

Down from the liquid heaven
　　In myftic order laid,
The white ftars rain at even
　　White joys that ne'er can fade :

For they rain on the folemn fpirit
  Mufing on things above,
On the realms that we inherit
  White with Eternal Love.

White in the Eafter feafon
  And at Chriftmas' time of joy,
Our Mother for loving reafon
  Ordaineth to employ.

White in the lovely May-tide
  Burfteth from every bufh ;
White in the face of beauty
  Frameth a maiden blufh.

White is the noon-tide glory
  Blanching the diftant hills ;
White on the ocean hoary
  The ftorm-toffed furges fills.

White is the Colour of Angels.

White are the fields at even
 When the frefh dew on them lies ;
White is the verge of heaven,
 Ere the fun begins to rife.

I loved a white-browed maiden
 Arched o'er with gold-brown hair,
And eyne with brightnefs laden
 As the brightnefs of fummer air.

O colour of white, I love thee !
 For ever amid my dreams
The fhadow of white-winged angels
 To guard me with watching feems.

GEORGE AKERS.

OUR LADY OF THE SNOWS.

I.

THE World is very foul and dark,
    And fin has marred its outline fair ;
But we are taught to look above
    And fee another image there !
And I will raife my eyes above,
    Above a World of fin and woe,
Where finlefs, grieflefs, near her Son
    Sits Mary on a Throne of fnow.

II.

Mankind feems very foul and dark
    In fome lights that we fee them in ;
Lo ! as the tide of life goes by,
    How many thoufands live in fin !

But I will raife my eyes above,
    Above the World's unthinking flow,
To where, fo human, yet fo fair,
    Sits Mary on her Throne of fnow.

III.

My heart is very foul and dark,
    Yes, ftrangely foul fometimes to me
Glare up the images of fin,
    My tempter loves to make me fee.
Then may I lift my eyes above,
    Above thefe paffions vile and low,
To where, in pleading contraft bright,
    Sits Mary on her Throne of fnow.

IV.

And oft that Throne, fo near our Lord's,
    To Earth fome of its radiance lends;
And Chriftians learn from her to fhun
    The path impure, that hell-ward tends:

For they have learnt to look above,
  Above the prizes here below,
To where, crowned with a ſtarry crown,
  Sits Mary on her Throne of ſnow.

v.

Bleſt be the whiteneſs of her Throne
  That ſhines ſo purely, grandly there,
With ſuch a paſſing glory bright,
  Where all is bright, and all is fair!
God, make me lift my eyes above,
  And love its holy radiance ſo,
That, ſome day, I may come where ſtill
  Sits Mary on her Throne of ſnow!

B.

"LET THE HILLS HEAR THY VOICE."

THE fun fhines bright and glorious, and the
    hill tops are illumed
    With a more than common light the day
    Our Lady was affumed ;
For her the cloudlefs blaze of noon on ·the lonely
    tarn is glowing,
And the many-founding torrents chant her praifes
    in their flowing.

For her the golden valleys thick with cornfields
    laugh and fing,
And with voices of innumerous birds the happy
    woodlands ring ;
The air is tremulous with fong, and a preternatural
    motion
Stirs the deep mufic of the waves in funlefs caves
    of Ocean ;

And the found of many waters with accord of
   folemn mirth,
Like a worfhip without words, goes up inceffant
   from the earth,
The Magnificat of mountain-ftreams, and—fweeteft
   after fhowers—
An odour as of frankincenfe, wafted from myrtle
   bowers.

And fhall we alone, dear Mother, when all around
   is gay,
Stand mute amid the tuneful choir that hails thy
   triumph day?
Nor heed the fkylark's matin hymn, flooding the
   heavens with praife,
Faint echo of their angel harps who on thy brightnefs gaze?

Shall thy children raife no anthem, all unaudienced
   though it be,

With the living rock for temple, and the far-
resounding sea,
Rolling organ notes of jubilee, responsive to their
song,
For the Mother of the Holy One, the Merciful, the
Strong?

What if there were who loved to roam those breezy
fern-clad hills,
And to dream away the summer nights beside their
tinkling rills;
Who thought to seek the beautiful in Earth's most
beauteous places,
While the mountain breath was fraught for them
with more than earthly graces;

Who revelled in the warm sunshine on lake and
flowery lea,
While Nature through her sweet constraints was
drawing them to thee?—

O fpeed them home, dear Mother-Maid, who linger
    on the way,
Lighten their eyes who cannot fee, and turn the
    feet that ftray!

Guide thou their weary fteps through days of anguifh
    and unreft,
Through the darknefs that is felt of doubts uncon-
    quered, unconfeft,
To the land beyond the Eaftern hills, lapt in the
    living ray
Of the Uncreated Vifion, where the fhadows flee
    away!

              Henry Nutcombe Oxenham.

THE SERVANT OF CHRIST.

"He that is called, being free, is Chriſt's ſervant."
1 *Cor.* vii. 22.

I.

THY Hands have made me! in ſoul-ſaving flood
Thy Heart poured forth for me its pre-
cious Blood,
And Thy ſweet Breath gave me its Life Divine;
Therefore, my God and Saviour! I am Thine!

II.

Thine by the mighty Maker's matchleſs art,
Thine by the Paſſion of His broken Heart,
Marked on my brow with the ſin-ſcaring ſign,
My God! my Saviour! ſoul and body Thine!

III.

Slave of my paſſions, by Thy Love ſet free,
Bound in eternal ſervitude to Thee,
Thy right in me yielded with glad accord,
The ſlave of Chriſt—the freeman of the Lord.

IV.

O glorious Love! that takes that outcaſt Name,
Once the ſad ſign of ſuffering and of ſhame,
And makes it, when for Chriſt man doth it bear,
Than Royal titles freer and more fair.

V.

Therefore, to render up to Thee above,
All the deep tender paſſion of my love,
All the poor ſervice that Thou wouldſt employ,
Is not alone my duty, but my joy!

VI.

And whatſoe'er I do, Lord ! let it be
Done from the heart—with ſingle eye to Thee :
My pureſt motive, and my beſt reward,
To be Chriſt's ſlave !—the freeman of the Lord !

JOHN S. B. MONSELL.

GOLDEN RAYS.

" Through Life's long day and death's dark night,
O gentle Jefu, be our Light."

F. W. Faber.

I.

WHEN tempefts ceafe at clofe of day,
    And evening is ferene,
    How welcome falls the golden ray
    O'er paftoral valleys feen—
As 'twere a meffage fent to cheer,
By miffioned angels lingering near.

II.

For, if a blinding mift of tears
    Awhile obfcured our fight,
The fadnefs of long-vanifhed years
    Seems like a dream of Night.

When, drawing near to Jordan's tide,
Glory illumes the other fide.

III.

The other fide?   What tongue may tell
   That orient blufh of Morn
Tinging the facred lilies' bell,
   And rofes without thorn.
Oh that we had thy wings, fair dove,
To foar and reft in bowers above!

IV.

The peace which this World cannot give
   And cannot take away
Is found when faithfully we ftrive
   God's precepts to obey:
Prepared to breaft the awful flood,
Supported on the Holy Rood.

v.

O wondrous mercy, thus to deign,
  And offer lasting rest,
From sorrow, wearinefs, and pain,
  On gentle Jefu's breast:
So may our Alleluias fweet
Adore the Blessed Paraclete!

C. A. M. W.

DREAMS.

I.

S childhood wanes our dreams become lefs
fair—
Heaven has gone farther off—the
child is dead :
When Manhood dawns upon us, it doth fcare
God's Mother from her watch befide our bed;
For I believe that o'er an infant's fleep
Our Lady doth a gentle vigil keep.

II.

Thus a child's flumber is a holy thing;
It deems its mother's kifs upon its brow
Is the foft glancing of an Angel's wing.—
Ah! I have no fuch graceful fancies now!
Therefore I hold, hearing of one who can
Dream like a little child,—Heaven loves that man.

JOHN PURCHAS.

"IN HOC SIGNO VINCE."

N the ancient ſtory,
   Once a warrior high
Saw a Croſs of glory
  Flaming in the ſky ;
While around it reaching,
  Writ by Hand Divine,
Ran the holy teaching,
  " Conquer by this ſign."

World and fleſh and devil
  Seek our deadly loſs,
We muſt fight with evil
  Strengthened by the Croſs ;
Thus our might renewing
  By the ſymbol bleſt,
" Faint but yet purſuing "
  Chriſt ſhall give us reſt.

Sign of our falvation
    Printed on the brow,
Ever frefh relation
    Of a folemn vow,
May we always love thee
    As our joy and pride,
Looking ftill above thee
    To the Crucified.

In the time of forrow
    Peaceful we fhall be,
Since from it we borrow
    Leffons, Lord, of Thee:
In the days of gladnefs
    We fhall do Thy will,
For Thy Crofs of fadnefs
    Keeps us humble ftill.

Till the cord is broken
    Of our earthly part,

Let us wear the token
    Near a loving heart :
When the eye is glazing
    With the final ftrife,
Still upon it gazing
    Pafs from death to Life.

ANGELUS DOMINI.

A PICTURE BY B. FRA ANGELICO.

PRESS each on each, sweet wings, and roof
    me in
    Some clos̄ed cell to hold my wearines̄—
Desired, as from unshadowed plains, to win
    The palmy gloaming of the oasis.

Soft wings, that floated ere the sun arose,
    Down pillared lines of ever-fruited trees,
Where through the many-gladed leafage flows
    The uncreated noon of Paradise.

Still wings, in contemplation oftentime
    Stretched on the ocean-depth that drowns desire,
Where lightening tides, in never-falling chime,
    Ring round the Angel isles in glass and fire.

From meadow lands that fleep beyond the ftars,
 From lilied woods and waves the Bleffed fee,
Pafs, bird of God, all pafs the golden bars,
 And in thy fair compaffion pity me.

O for the garden-city of the Flower,
 Of jewelled Italy the chofen gem,
Where angels and Giotto dreamed a tower
 In lovelinefs of New Jerufalem.

For thefe, when roseate as a wingëd cloud
 Upon the faffron of the paling Eaft,
A glowing pillar in the Houfe of God,
 That tower arofe, the very lovelieft :

Then fhaking wings and voices there that fang
 Pafs up and down the chafëd jafper wall,
And through the cryftal traceries outrang,
 As when from height to deep the feraphs call.

O for the valley-flopes which Arno cleaves
    With arrowy heads of gold unceafingly,
Parting the twilight of the grey-green leaves,
    As fhafted sun-gleam on a rain-cloud fky.

For there, more white than mifts of bloom above
    When funfet kindles Luni's vineyard height,
Strange prefences have paced the olive grove,
    And dazed the cyprefs cloifter into light.

But not for me the angel-haunted fouth—
    I fpread my hands acrofs the unlovely plain,
I faint for beauty in the daily drouth
    Of beauty, as the fields for Auguft rain.

Yet hope is mine againft fome eaftern dawn,
    Not in a vifion, but reality,
To fee thy wings, and, in thine arms upborne,
    To reft me in a fairer Italy.

                  DIGBY MACKWORTH DOLBEN.

THE CHILD'S OFFERING.

WAS feſtal day in Heaven,
  And many a feraph came
With many a coſtly offering
  To bleſs the Eternal Name.

On never-tiring wings
  Of burning love they flew,
Cleaving their eager upward way
  Through the cærulean blue.

Swift as the lightning's ray,
  Which from the fartheſt Eaſt
Darts forth a beam of radiant flame
  Unto the fartheſt Weſt :

So, ſwiftly from each realm
  Of wide Creation's bound,
The willing vaſſals gladly throng
  The dazzling throne around :

Each meekly veils his face
    Beneath the fhadowing wing,
Before the awful Majefty
    Of the Everlafting King:

Each bearing to his Lord
    Some mark of tribute meet ;
Some fplendid fervice, to be laid
    Low at his Sovereign's feet.

One brings a virgin world,
    Whofe habitations fair
And finlefs, happy denizens
    Entrufted to his care,

He has preferved from harm—
    Has trained in holy fear ;
And now again refigns his charge,
    Meet for the Vifion clear.

One leads in ponderous chains
   A countlefs hoft of hell
Whom he has vanquifhed in the fight
   With Lucifer who fell.

One tells that he has hung
   In diftant fields of space
A galaxy of rolling funs
   For angels' dwelling-place.

One wakes to a new ftrain
   The mufic of the fpheres ;—
Rich harmonies till now unheard
   E'en by celeftial ears.

Then all in chorus join,
   Raifing a lofty fong ;—
A theme of praife which never yet
   Has fired archangel's tongue.

Yet, 'mid the fhining train
　　Of bending Cherubin,
Is one whofe offering prevails
　　A fpecial grace to win:

He brings no fpotlefs world,
　　No fpoils of victory;
He leads not with his voice or harp
　　The minftrelfy on high:

He bears no royal gift
　　Nor coftly facrifice;
Of paltry worth it would be held
　　If weighed at this World's price:

Yet 'tis as rich and rare,
　　In fight of Heaven's King,
As all the trophies of fuccefs
　　Which flaming feraphs bring.

'Tis the firſt heavenward throb
  Of a young heart's young love ;
Its freſh, full tide of gratitude
  To Him Who dwells above.

Grateful as Spring's firſt flowers,
  Lovely as earlieſt dawn,
Precious as in a mother's eyes
  Her infant eldeſt-born ;

Pure as the deep blue lake
  Which, 'neath the ſummer ſky,
Mirrors the azure and the gold,
  Unruffled by a ſigh :

So dear in Jeſus' ſight,
  So beautiful appears
The heart which gives itſelf to Him
  In childhood's opening years.

WILLIAM EDWARD GREEN.

A DREAM OF PARADISE.

I N the myſtic realm of ſlumber, in the quiet
    land of reſt,
    Came to me a radiant viſion of the Coun-
      try of the Bleſt ;
Angels, through the ſilvery moonbeams, gliding
    ſwiftly from the ſkies,
Brought to me from Eden's garden that fair Dream
    of Paradiſe.

Foremoſt in a long proceſſion, in her ſhining raiment
    dreſt,
Came the one who, through all ages, bears a name
    for ever bleſt ;
Queen of Heaven ! Spotleſs Lily ! walking in re-
    ſplendent light

Which no mortal eyes can fathom, in the boundlefs
 Infinite ;
Bleffed Lady ! Mother Glorious ! dare I hope to fee
 thy face
In the Land where none can enter, fave through the
 redeeming grace
Of the Crofs which gives us accefs into the Moft
 Holy Place ?

Thofe who in her fteps had trodden, followed her, in
 robes of white ;
Palms within their hands were waving, they were
 crowned with gems of light.

They were there, the martyr-maidens, who had con-
 quered in the ftrife ;
They were there, the meek and patient, who had
 borne the Crofs through life ;
Ranfomed from Earth's tribulation—fafe for ever in
 the Fold ;

Paffing 'neath the pearly gateway,—walking in the
    ftreets of gold ;
And I heard their thrilling anthem floating o'er the
    cryftal fea—
" Unto Him Who hath redeemed us, Glory, Praife,
    and Honour be ! "

But the dazzling vifion faded—it was far too bright
    to ftay ;
In the rofy tints of dawning vanifhed the celeftial ray.
Earthly chains are ftill around us, mortal prayers we
    ftill muft pray,
Pilgrims in the land of exile—waiting till the perfect
    day
Breaks upon the diftant mountains, and the fhadows
    flee away.

HELEN MONTAGU STUART.

THE BREAD OF LIFE.

HEN by Thine altar, Lord, I kneel,
　　And think upon Thy love,
　O make my heart Thy goodnefs feel,
　　Fix it on things above:
My dearest Lord, when I retrace
　Thy wondrous love for me;
Oh, how can I affection place
　On anything but Thee?

About to leave this wretched Earth,
　On man Thy thoughts ftill bent,
Thy facred boundlefs love gave birth
　To this fweet Sacrament:
　　My dearest Lord, when I retrace
　　　Thy wondrous love for me;
　　Oh, how can I affection place
　　　On anything but Thee?

O Manna, which my fovereign Lord
 In pity left for me,
Without this majefty adored
 What would this exile be ?
  My deareft Lord, when I retrace
   Thy wondrous love for me;
  Oh, how can I affection place
   On anything but Thee ?

A defert land of woe and care,
 A pilgrimage of ftrife,
Who could its griefs and trials bear
 Without this Bread of Life ?
  My deareft Lord, when I retrace
   Thy wondrous love for me ;
  Oh, how can I affection place
   On anything but Thee ?

My foul here finds a fovereign balm—
 A cure for every grief,

Mid care and pain a heavenly calm,
  A folace and relief.
      My deareft Lord, when I retrace
        Thy wondrous love for me ;
      Oh, how can I affection place
        On anything but Thee ?

Supported by this Heavenly Bread,
  My Lord's laft pledge of Love,
With joy the rugged path I'll tread
  To Horeb's mount above.
      My deareft Lord, when I retrace
        Thy wondrous love for me ;
      Oh, how can I affection place
        On anything but Thee ?

Strengthened by this, my foul its flight
  Shall from this exile foar,
To dwell in realms of blifs and light
  For ever—evermore.

My dearest Lord, when I retrace
Thy wondrous love for me;
Oh, how can I affection place
On anything but Thee?

RIVER THOUGHTS.

ON RECEIVING FROM AN OLD AND DEAR FRIEND

A BEAUTIFUL BOOK ON THE THAMES.

 TEMPLE,[1] backed with tree and bafed
    with turf,
Crefting the bright blue reach : —an
    ancient Lock,[2]
On whofe worn gates the tiny wavelets knock
For entrance, and play round with mimick furf :

A Cell, once of religion—then of rakes,[3]
And now of pleafure-feaftings underneath

---

[1] The Temple or fummer-houfe on Fawley Ifland below
Henley.
[2] Hambledon Lock.
[3] Medmenham Abbey—and its " Francifcans."

Old Trees, through which the river-breezes breathe,
And found of voice and flute fweet mufic makes

From fhallop, hafting homeward at grey eve :
White cliffs :[1] broad fall of waters at the Ford,[2]
Dove-cote, and Terrace-walk of foft green fward,[3]
Then an old Abbey,[4] where a Boy[5] would weave
Fancies[6]—afloat and drifting to and fro—
Wild fancies—that fhall live while Thames' ftill
     waters flow.

     Such is the fong that Memory fings
         To me of homes and hours gone by ;
      A tale of ne'er-forgotten things ;
         A record that will never die :

---

[1] Danesfield Cliffs.

[2] Harley-ford, its falls and foot-bridge.

[3] Hurley: Dove-cote and waterfide walk, Lady-place.

[4] Bifham.   [5] Shelley.

[6] " The Revolt of Iflam," under its paft name, " Laon and Cythna."

Stirred by thofe feven fweet myftic ftrings
Up, from the inmoft heart, it fprings—
The thought—that all Life's bygone brings
      Back to the eye ;
Old hearts, old haunts, old talks, old times,
Old Halls, old Towers, and old Church-chimes,
      Life's melody.

WILLIAM JOHN BLEW.

PURBROOK, HAMPSHIRE.

O EASTWARD ſpeed in gentle thought,
    And climb the ſteep Portſdown,
Then the meek rivulet be ſought
    That winds beyond its crown :
As weſtwards tends the ſunlight, round
    On church and hamlet look,
And muſe how meetly this fair ground
    Is named from this Pure Brook.

This Brook is like the chriſtened ſouls
    Who in fair Purbrook dwell ;
The river-wave, the life-wave, rolls
    Each from a ſecret well ;
But men may mark the ſtreamlet's birth
    Where wild birds build and ſing ;
Who may trace back the Church on earth ?
    Who ſhall declare its ſpring ?

Wilt trace it to the font's fair gleam,
 Pure water purified,
Pure water from an earthly ſtream
 Loſt in a purer tide ?
There with the Everlaſting Years
 Is linked the life late given ;
There is no eye of ſun-lit ſpheres
 Gifted to pierce the Heaven.

Glaſſing the Sun upon its breaſt,
 Gladdening the neighbour ſoil,
The ſtream, ſcarce noticed, flows to reſt,
 'Twixt the green banks of toil.
This is each faithful blood-bought ſoul,
 They who ſtill heav'nward look
To ſeek their being's Fount and Goal,
 To liſt their own Pure Brook.

A. MIDDLEMORE MORGAN.

HYMN AFTER HOLY COMMUNION.

H union wonderful and true !
  Oh, Love ! oh, blifs beyond compare !
What can the heart enraptured do
  When God Himfelf is there ?

After communion what is earth ?
  Life feems indeed but vanity :
Its brighteft hours are never worth
  One moment fpent with Thee.

This moment does the work of years,
  The foul hath drunk a joy fo deep
That fhe may bid farewell to tears,
  Such as Earth's children weep.

Jefus ! be Thou my hidden reft,
  Reign over me fupreme, alone ;
The deareft wifh within my breaft
  Is to be all Thine Own !

And now, if to my daily ſtrife
   I muſt return, and bear my part ;
Do Thou, my Lord, my Light, my Life,
   Keep to Thyſelf my heart !

Hold it, that it may never ſtray,
   Loſt in a World of ſin and care,
Fix it in the unerring way
   Of diſcipline and prayer.

Give me Thy bleſſing, Lord, again ;
   And I will fight beneath Thine Eye,
And win, perchance, through days of pain,
   A glorious victory.

H

SALVE MI ANGELICE.

A HYMN FOR THE COMMEMORATION OF GUARDIAN ANGELS.

HAIL! my guardian ſpirit, hail!
 Angel ever bleſſed,
  Who of light within the veil
   Throughly art poſſeſſed ;
Thou of God Almighty haſt
 Beatific viſion,
Sweet for ever to the taſte,
 Unalloyed fruition.

When the ſpirits proud were caſt
 Into death undying,
Thee did God eſtabliſh faſt,
 Heavenly grace ſupplying :

In His paths preferved thee,
   Spirit true and tender,
And commiffioned thee to be
   My weak foul's defender.

Therefore I with bended knee
   Bow myfelf before thee,
And upraifing fuppliantly
   Heart and hands, implore thee,
That, with ever-watchful art,
   Thou to-day wouldft aid me,
Left the adverfary's dart
   Subtly fhould invade me.

May my body from diftrefs
   Be by thee protected,
Be all thoughts of wickednefs
   From my mind rejected :

Everywhere and always fpeed
From the foe to hide me,
And in thought and word and deed
Be at hand to guide me.

Cleanfe all paft and prefent faults
From my mind's intention,
And, when evil next affaults,
Grant thy intervention.
O confole and care for me,
Cherifh me in trouble,
Purge, enlighten perfectly,
And my zeal redouble.

Pray that I remiffion find
Of the Judge's fentence,
So to fhare my joy of mind
On my true repentance ;

Living as ſhall pleaſe Him beſt
   Unto my life's cloſing,
All my longings aye at reſt,
   All on Him repoſing.

In the hour of death, beſtow
   Thy true conſolation ;
Shield me from the watchful foe,
   Bid me take my ſtation,
Where the hoſts of heaven among
   In God's courts attending,
I may join the praiſes ſung
   To His Name unending.   Amen.

H. W. MOZLEY.

A LEGEND OF THE WEEPING
WILLOW.

WHITE were the ſtairs of marble ſtone,
   But whiter were His Feet,
   Flecked with the Blood that muſt atone
For the apple ſickly-ſweet ;
   As He came down,
   Each mocking clown
Aroſe the King to greet.

It was not yet the time of figs,
   But trees were budding fair,
They ſtripped the lithe long willow-twigs,—
   All things the crime muſt ſhare !—
   With rod and ſcourge
   Their guilt to purge
Whoſe ſins the Sinleſs bare.

And red ftains mar the marble ftone,
    And on the long green leaves
Are blood-drops, as the willow lone
    Still hangs its head and grieves
        By pool and flood,
        Where the pale blue bud
    The wreath of Memory weaves.

B. Montgomerie Ranking.

THE HOLY SOULS.

"The Souls of the righteous are in the Hands of God."

ORD of the living and the dead,
 Thy children feek Thine aid
For Souls who, in Thy Juftice dread,
 Suffer for debts unpaid.

Shut out from Thee their one fole Love,
 They alway languifh fore
For cooling ftreams of blifs above,
 And Heaven's wide-opened door.

In twilight gloom they patient wait,
 Crofs-bearers of their Lord;
Stricken, until the prifon-gate
 Be opened at Thy word.

Not yet fo cleanfed and purified
   That they may fee Thy Face:
Not yet made meet, by fuffering tried,
   For Thine all-pure embrace.

Yet Thou doft love them, and Thy love
   Is blifs amid their woe,
And for Thy fake the joys above
   They readily forego.

O then make hafte, good Chrift! and hear
   Our *De-profundis* cry;
'Releafe the Souls, to Thee fo dear,
   Who patient waiting lie.

Refrefh them parched, with gracious rains—
   They long and thirft for Thee;—
Unloofe their bonds, remit their pains,
   And fet Thy captives free.

Low at Thine altars here we bow,
 With tears Thy Paſſion plead,
The ſpotleſs Victim lifted now
 We offer for their need.

Soon give them welcome up above
 In Home of bliſsful reſt,
Fruition of Eternal Love,
 And ſight of Viſion bleſt.

E. LOUISA LEE.

THE TROUVÈRE.[1]

 MAKE not songs, but only find :—
    Love, following still the circling sun,
His carols cast on every wind,
    And other singer is there none !

I follow Love, though far he flies :
    I sing his song, at random found,
Like plume some bird of Paradise
    Drops, passing, on our dusky bound.

In some, methinks, at times there glows
    The passion of a heavenlier sphere :
These, too, I sing :—but sweeter those
    I dare not sing, and faintly hear.

AUBREY DE VERE.

---

[1] The Greeks called the poet " the Maker."   In the middle ages, some of the best poets took a more modest title—that of " the Finder."

HYMN OF PRAISE.

(Pſalm cxlviij.)

PRAISE, O praiſe the Lord of Heaven,
    Praiſe Him, praiſe Him in the height ;
Sun and moon, for ever praiſe Him,
    Praiſe Him, all ye ſtars and light.

Praiſe Him, praiſe Him, all His angels,
    Praiſe Him, praiſe Him, all His hoſt :
Praiſe the God of our Salvation,
    Father, Son, and Holy Ghoſt !

Praiſe Him, praiſe Him, all ye Heavens,
    And ye waters, that above,
From your everlaſting fountains,
    Riſe in light and fall in love.

Praife Him, all ye deeps and dragons
  Upon earth, praife ye the Lord;
Fire and hail and fnow and vapour,
  Wind and ftorm, fulfil His Word.

Praife Him, all ye hills and mountains,
  Cedars fair and fruitful trees,
Beafts and cattle, birds and infects,
  Morning's light and evening's breeze.

Let them praife His Name Moft Holy,
  For He fpake and they were made,
Laws which never fhall be broken,
  Deep in their foundations laid.

Kings below and all the people,
  Princes, judges of the earth,
Young and old men, maidens, children,
  Praife His Name of matchlefs worth.

For that Name, all names excelling,
  From His people's hearts ſhall raiſe
To His own eternal dwelling
  Endleſs ſongs of love and praiſe.

Praiſe, O praiſe the Lord of Heaven,
  Praiſe Him, praiſe Him in the height;
Sun and moon, for ever praiſe Him,
  Praiſe Him, all ye ſtars and light!

Praiſe Him, praiſe Him, all His angels,
  Praiſe Him, praiſe Him, all His hoſt:
Praiſe the God of our ſalvation,
  Father, Son, and Holy Ghoſt.

JOHN S. B. MONSELL.

THE SHIP IN THE STORM.

" The ſhip was now in the midſt of the ſea, toſſed
with waves."

 SAW " the waves of this troubleſome
world," raging and dark and cold,—
Oh, who will guide in the ſtormy tide to
reſt in the city of gold?

The Lord has been to our realms of ſin, and bought
us in Heaven a ſhare,

But He is gone back on the angel's track, and how
ſhall we reach Him there?

Then a glance I caſt through the long, long paſt;
(its viſta was nearly dark,)

And, through the haze of vaniſhed days, diſcerned a
noble barque

Which the " Carpenter's Son," that fearleſs One,
had built with His own right hand,

And in her thoſe dear to His Heart while here,
embarked for their Fatherland.

The Workman is gone, yet crowds preſs on to that
    fruit of His toil unpriced ;

All bear the ſign of Love Divine, the holy Croſs of
    Chriſt.

The ſame ſweet Light through ſtorm and night is
    guiding all to reſt,

And, hand-in-hand, to toil for land, they ſhould be
    ſurely bleſt.

But ſome cannot view the lantern true, and to them
    all days are dark ;

Some proudly rear, and think as clear, their candle's
    little ſpark.

Some try to wile the brief ſummer's ſmile for ever
    there to roam,—

Alas ! to ſuch is the voyage much, and little worth
    their home.

Some look for light with aching ſight, and tremble
    day by day,

Leſt, though they ſtrive to ſafe arrive, they ſhould
    be caſt away.

Some leave the reſt, and boldly breaſt alone the open
    wave,

And many die from far and nigh, and find an ocean
    grave;

Like drops of rain on the ſtormy main, their place is
    known no more,—

O death and life! O toil and ſtrife! when will
    this ſcene be o'er?

Y. N.

CORPORATE REUNION.

 LORD, we know that all who love Thy
   Name
   Are one in Thee; Thy Spirit's quick-
    ening fire
Has wrapt their torpid nature into flame,
   And given them oneneſs of intenſe deſire
   To mount towards Thee higher ſtill and higher.
Yet are they widely ſevered to their ſhame
   In outward worſhip : diſcord in the choir
Brings on their glorious Faith the ſceptic's blame.
O turn we, therefore, ſchiſm-torn to Thee,
   And aſk that Thou wouldſt make us whole again,
Not only in the Spirit's unity,
   But in a viſible communion ;—then
The Holy Catholic Church indeed will be
   Thy home, Thy tabernacle among men.

JOHN CHARLES EARLE.

Viſitation of B. V. Mary, 1878.

SUPER FLUMINA.

THE vefper bell is pealing foft,
 And I know that, far away,
 The vefper hymn goes up aloft,
 To lull the dying day ;
And a gentle Child on bended knee
Is pouring forth a prayer for me.

Pray, gentle fpirit, far away,
 By that fweet fouthern fea ;
I have need enough that day by day
 Some prayer fhould rife for me,
Some incenfe to the eternal fhrine,
From heart and lips as pure as thine.

I fcarce could pray an hour ago,
 A weight was on my heart,

But now it melts like morning fnow,
   And I can weep apart,
For thou art praying for me now,
And God will liften to thy vow.

Pray, gentle fpirit; prayer of mine
   Is ftained and flecked with earth,
But every fnow-white prayer of thine
   Is rich with Angel's worth;
And mingling in the ftarry zone,
Thofe prayers fhall purify mine own.

Sweet is the Ave-Mary bell,
   In Mary's land of love,
And fweet the vefper hymns that fwell
   To Her dear Throne above;
And fweet to me far, far away,
The hour when Mary's children pray.

Adieu, fweet Child, adieu to-night!
   Chrift keep thee fafe from ill!

Thy dreams be fweet, thy fleep be light,
    Good Angels guard thee ftill :
And God the Father from above
Smile on thee with a Father's love.

FOLLIOTT S. PIERPOINT.

IMMACULATA.

OULD fhe, that Deftined one, could fhe
    On whom His gaze was fixed for aye,
  Tranfgrefs like Eve, partake that Tree,
In turn the Serpent's dupe and prey?

Had He no Pythian fhaft that hour,
  Her Son—her God—to pierce the Foe
That ftrove her greatnefs to devour,
  Eclipfe her glories? Deem not fo!

O Mary! in that Firft Decree
  He faw the affailer, fent the aid :—
Filial it was, His love for thee
  Ere thou wert born ; ere worlds were made.

One Innocence on earth remained
  By Grace divine, not Nature's worth,
And welcomed—through His Blood, unſtained—
  Redeeming Sanctity to earth.

                  AUBREY DE VERE.

ANOTHER FLEETING DAY IS GONE.

ANOTHER fleeting day is gone,—
    Slow o'er the Weſt the ſhadows riſe;
    Swiftly ſoft ſtealing hours have flown,
And Night's dark mantle veils the ſkies.

Another fleeting day is gone,—
    Swept from the records of the year,
And ſtill with each ſucceſſive ſun
    Life's fading viſions diſappear.

Another fleeting day is gone,—
    When all who in God's care confide
As their appointed work is done,
    Reſt in His love at eventide.

Another fleeting day is gone,—
    But ſoon a fairer day ſhall riſe,

A day whofe never-fetting fun
   Shall pour its light o'er cloudlefs fkies.

Another fleeting day is gone,—
   All praife to God, as is moft meet,
To God the Father, God the Son,
   And God th' all-holy Paraclete.   Amen.

                      I.

IN GOD'S SIGHT.

WHY ſhould we vex our fooliſh minds
So much from day to day,
With what concerning us an idle World
May think or ſay?

Do we not know there ſits a Judge,
Before Whoſe ſearching eyes
Our inmoſt hidden being cleft in twain
And open lies?

O my Omniſcient Lord and God!
Enough, enough for me,
That Thou the evil in me and the good
Doſt wholly ſee.

Let others in their fancies deem of me,
Or ſay, whate'er they will,
Such as I am before Thy judgment-throne
So am I ſtill.

Praife they my good beyond defert,
    And all my bad ignore ;—
That am I which in Thy pure fight I am,
    No lefs, no more !

Decry they all my good, and blame
    My evil in excefs ;—
That am I which in Thy pure fight I am,
    No more, no lefs !

EDWARD CASWALL.

"THY KINGDOM COME."

No. I.

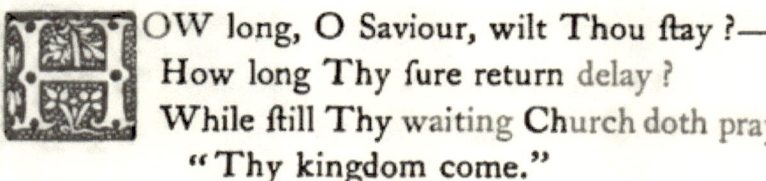OW long, O Saviour, wilt Thou ſtay ?—
How long Thy ſure return delay ?
While ſtill Thy waiting Church doth pray
  "Thy kingdom come."

Didſt not Thou teach the prayer, O Lord ?
Haſt Thou not paſſed the faithful word ?
Oh ! gird Thee with Thy conquering ſword :
  " Thy kingdom come."

Are not the realms of Earth Thine own ?
Come, then, and ſtabliſh here Thy throne :
In all the World reign Thou alone :
  " Thy kingdom come."

Jefu ! defcend again from high ;
And while Thine armies fill the fky
Let Earth refound, and Heaven reply :
 " Thy kingdom come."

Why lingereth Thy chariot ftill ?
When wilt Thou all the nations fill
With the glad praife of Sion's hill ?
 " Thy kingdom come."

Till then, oh ! keep us in the way
Which leadeth to Eternal Day ;
And grant us grace in faith to fay :
 " Thy kingdom come."

WILLIAM EDWARD GREEN.

"THY KINGDOM COME."

No. II.

S AY not that hours are lonelier now and
darker
  Than days were dark of yore,
Say not that wild winds moan old days' departure,
  For funfhine lights the floor :

Yes, golden funfhine creeps through pane and portal
  Up the dim wall,
Whence pictured faces look with fmiling feature,
  And voices feem to call :

Sunfhine of Earth, bright type of heavenly glory,
  Where come nor lofs nor fears,—
Sunfhine of Earth, flecked ever with dark fhadows,
  In this fad vale of tears.

Round us fuch fhades have deepened, paled the
    gloaming,
    Now Summer **joys have fled,**
Yet even in Winter come familiar greetings
    And memories of the **dead.**

Until we pafs, in Spring, **Life's June, or Winter,**
    From this ftrange varying fcene,
Bind us to thofe we loved, **by** living prayer-bonds,
    Lord, keep their memories green :

Grey hairs **and deep-veined fingers, cold and death-**
    ftruck,
    With **De** *profundis* fung,
Faces fo white and calm, the ftruggle over,
    When chimes of hope were rung :

While round the death-biers little children fearful
    Gathered **with** fmile and tear,

And little palms were joined in interceſſion
  For thoſe ſo loved and dear.

Paſt all the woes and ſufferings, o'er the ſtruggle,
  No more the trumpet-call :
Paſt all the toil and all the ſtrong temptation,
  No weakneſs now, no fall.

As pants the hart for cool refreſhing brooklets,
  When heated in the chaſe,
So long the ſouls, O Lord, of our departed
  To look upon Thy Face.

Patient and waiting for glad ſtreaks of ſunlight
  To ſcare dark miſts away,
Patient and waiting through the long night-watches
  For God's all-peaceful day.

There bonds long-ſevered, with ſad ſeparations,
  By His divine decree,

Shall be new-linked in that true home celeſtial
  Before the cryſtal ſea.

So ‚when bright ſpring-flowers gild the glad green
      meadows,
  And birds rejoicing ſing,
Pray for the Reſurrection-morning's beauty—
  Look for the Church's King.

Or here, when Autumn's reddening touch ſo
      changeth
  Leaf, floweret-bloom, and lea,
Aſk we to tread the good God's garden homewards,
  And eat of Life's rich Tree.

We ſtill miſs friends, and grieve o'er their departure,
  Hands cold and voices dumb,—
Join us anew where ſeparations are not,
  O Lord, Thy Kingdom come !

So, as at sleeping-place, poor pilgrim-strangers,
    Thine Own loved Prayer we pray,
We look back from the empty tomb of Easter,
    On to the breaking Day.

FREDERICK GEORGE LEE.

THE TWO CROWNS.

 MADE myfelf a myrtle crown ;
　　 I crowned myfelf with leaves and
　　　　 flowers ;
　 All day I lay in rofy bowers,
　 All day till the fweet fun went down.

The myrtle withered on my head,
　 My crown became a crown of pain,
　 I could not pluck it off again,
With thofe dead leaves my heart feemed dead.

All night, all night, without relief,
　 I wandered, while the ftars were bright,
　 I wandered all that weary night,
And all my foul was fick with grief.

But when then morning broke once more,
   And all the hills were rofy fair,
   I found a ruined chapel there,
I paffed the little chancel door :

The Holy Altar glittered cold,
   Altar and Crofs were broken all,
   The mofs was thick upon the wall,
The day-fpring tinged its tufts with gold.

I knelt before the broken fhrine,
   I could not fpeak for fobs and tears,
   I could not pray for wildering fears,
The ruin of that fane was mine.

Long, long I knelt in my defpair,
   But when the fun in heaven was high,
   A glory feemed to hover by,
I felt a Healing Prefence there.

So, when my grief was calmer grown,
   I faid, "My heart was dark within;
   O God, I finned a deadly fin,
I finned, to wear the myrtle crown."

I faw a Form of Beauty there,
   A Form of Beauty heavenly bright,
   A glorious Form of awful light,
A Form of Beauty faireft-fair.

I wept, and clafped His facred Feet,
   I wept and kiffed them, as I lay:
   He took my crown of pain away:
I wept, and all my tears were fweet.

Another crown I wear ev'n now,
   A fweeter crown than in thofe bowers,
   And part are Amaranthine flowers,
And part are thorns from His dear Brow.

FOLLIOTT S. PIERPOINT.

EVENTIDE.

WHISPER the angel voices foft and kind,
　　More gentle than the fummer even's wind
　　　　That murmurs playful o'er the deep,—
"Sleep, child of earth," they fay, "now take thy reft;
The twilight darkens in the glowing weft,
　Spirits around thee watch fhall keep."

Come floating on the breath of balmy air,
Sweet dreams of heaven, and of our loved ones there,
　For ever in their Father's keep.
And whilft ftill Night ftole on with filent tread,
Around me hovering, holy Angels faid,
　"He giveth His beloved fleep."

And comes anon, from yonder wooded hill,
The diftant murmur of fome hidden rill

That ripples down its ftony bed.
And yet again I hear the angels' fong,
By evening's dying breezes borne along,
  " Sleep, fleep, ftill darknefs reigns o'erhead.

" Reft, reft," I ftill hear wafted on the breeze,
That, fighing fadly through the fhadowy trees,
  Makes mufic always low and deep—
And comes once more the oft-repeated ftrain,
Re-echoed gently from yon darkening main,
  " He giveth His beloved fleep."

                              HEDLEY VICARS.

HYMN FOR ALL SAINTS' DAY.

E give Thee thanks, O Lord our God,
For all the Saints Thy path who trod—
The path of pain, the path of death,
The path of Him Who triumpheth.

For they have braved the hour of ſhame,
The croſs, the rack, the cord, the flame,
The dagger and the cup of woe,
If only Jeſus they might know.

All this they counted not for loſs,
For they were ſoldiers of the Croſs:
They recked not of the grief or pain,
If only Jeſus they might gain.

He is their Saviour, He their Lord,
He their exceeding great reward;

Though loft be all that fills our cares,
If Him they have, then all is theirs.

From us their forms have paffed away—
Mere viewlefs fpirits, mouldering clay—
Some live upon the life of fame,
Some leave no veftige but a name.

But when fhall found the trump of doom,
To call the tenants of the tomb,
A mighty army they fhall ftand,
Arrayed in white at God's Right Hand.

A mighty hoft, to man unknown,
In glory ranged around the Throne ;
He knows His own Who ruled the ftrife—
Their names are in the Book of Life.

GERARD MOULTRIE.

THE GREAT CLOUD OF WITNESSES.

"Compaſſed about with ſo great a cloud of witneſſes."—St.
Paul.
"I believe in the Communion of Saints."—*Apoſtles' Creed.*

GONE for them the time of ſorrow, paſſed
 for ever toil and pain,
 Weeping eyes and weary ſpirits, ſtumbling
 feet, or moil or ſtain ;
No more death nor ſin can touch them, they are
 ſafely folded now,
Great the guerdon of their patience, bright the crowns
 upon their brow.

Once, like us, they knew of weakneſs, of temptation's
 power, and ſhame,
But their God was near to help them, for they
 truſted in His Name ;
So victoriouſly they triumphed, though, like us, in
 war they ſtrove,

Now they gaze upon His beauty, Who, like them,
  we ſtrive to love.

But, though rapt in ceaſeleſs worſhip, round the
  Lamb's high throne in light,
Though impaſſible exultant, bathed in fathomleſs
  delight ;
Still from out the golden bulwarks, where the angels
  throng around,
Mark they well our faltering footſteps as we march
  through hoſtile ground.

Mindful are they of our victories when from ſin we
  turn away,
When, our burdens laid aſide, we walk as children of
  the day :
Yes, they yearn with love for ſinners, long to greet
  thoſe exiles dear,
And to ſhare with them the laurels when the fight
  is ended here.

Aſk we then their prayers to aid us—know they not
    the gifts we need?

Who on earth being ſtrong to battle, ſtill are ſtrong
    to intercede:

Filled while here with love's compaſſion, pity now
    for each they know;

Seek we then their willing ſuccour, help to triumph
    o'er the foe.

He will hear them, Who has promiſed, " What ye aſk
    ye ſhall receive;"

And His grace ſhall flow upon us who in His ſure
    word believe;

Bound and bonded in communion with each other
    and the Trine,

Where the light is ever luſtrous, and the peace is all
    divine.

The Authoreſs of " THE DEPARTED
AND OTHER VERSES."

UNKNOWN GRAVES.

THE grafs is rank, the fhades are deep,
  Where the unknown their flumber keep,
  The early funlight, faffron-new,
Scarce fmites the grafs or gilds the dew ;—
Unprayed for, tended not, they wait,
Thofe Holy Souls, outfide God's Gate.

Beyond the Church's northern wall
Only day's noon-tide glories fall,
Here—dawn and morn, foft eve, dark night
Above—no change, unfading light ;
Yet round glide angel-guardians nigh
To hear a plaint and heed a figh.

No croffes mark thofe northern graves,
No flowers adorn, no yew-tree waves ;

Unknown, uncared for, there they lie,
Under the chill of wintry fky,
Or, under light of July's fun,
Lorn and forgotten every one.

Pafs no lone namelefs fleeper's bed,
For once on fuch Heaven's dew was fhed:
By fudden death, by wafting pain,
God called them to Himfelf again:
Pray then for Souls who longing wait
To enter Sion's golden gate.

The grafs is rank, deep fhadows lie
Under charged cloud or golden fky;
Not by the Church's fouthern plot
Where rofe blooms with forget-me-not,
But for all Souls whofe bodies reft
Under the northern churchyard's breaft.

When chimes for mafs ring out at morn
O'er fnow-clothed vales or ripening corn,

Gather within the open door
God's dews of mercy to implore
For Souls unknown, in Chriſt new-born,
Waiting, unprayed for, lone and lorn.

FREDERICK GEORGE LEE.

Littlemore, September, 1874.

MANET SABBATISMUS.

WHEN man abode in Paradiſe,
    There was in gardens once
    A perfect reſt defying price ;
But man, ſo eager to be wiſe,
  Hath proved himſelf a dunce,
    That toileth ſtill and ſtraineth :
    And yet a reſt remaineth.

The ſerpent dwelt in Paradiſe,
  A good beaſt and a kindly,
But Satan coming, tempter-wiſe,
Filled all the poor beaſt's mouth with lies,
  And Eve ſhe liſtened blindly ;
    And living-kind complaineth :
    And yet a reſt remaineth.

By wells of water, where the trees
   Bow down to kifs the flowers
That, anchored, rock in morning breeze,
And fpread their filver chalices
   To catch the morning fhowers,
     No final reft man gaineth :
     And yet a reft remaineth.

In tender voice, in fong of bird,
   In pfaltery's foft rhyming,—
So fweet becaufe more felt than heard,—
   In found of kiffes, timing
   The hours that afk no chiming,
     There is no reft : earth waneth :
     Only the reft remaineth :

Remaineth in a garden-ground
   Where groweth Rofe and Lily,
Remaineth where the waters found,

Where never winds blow chilly,
Nor harfh voice echoes fhrilly,
Where the Rofe-lily reigneth,
There the true reft remaineth !

A little while, a little heat,
A little lonelinefs,—
And endlefs time that grows more fweet,
And warmth with no diftrefs,
And fellowfhip to blefs
His reft who reft obtaineth :
The final reft remaineth.

B. MONTGOMERIE RANKING.

COMPLINE HYMN.

OME, bleſt **Redeemer** of the Earth,
Shew to the **World** a **Virgin-Birth,**
Let all the wondering ages know
Which birth befeems our God below.

Not of the feed of mortal race,
By myftic Breath of heavenly grace,
The Word of God, in flefh arrayed,
True offspring blooms of Mother-maid.

The Virgin bears the Burthen pure,
And Ever-virgin doth endure ;
Like pennon bright her graces fhine,
And God is in His hallowed fhrine.

The Bridegroom from His chamber fprings,
Meet palace of the King of kings,
True God, true Man, in Perfon One,
Like giant glad His courfe to run.

From Sire in Heaven He goeth forth,
To live in Heaven returns from Earth,
Defcending e'en to Hell's abode,
Afcending to the Throne of God.

Eternal Sire's co-equal Son,
Thy flefhly girdle gird Thee on,
The frailty of our mortal plight
To ftrengthen with immortal might.

Full brightly fhines Thy manger-bed,
And Night herfelf new light doth fhed,
A Light on which no night fhall clofe,
Aye bright to Faith as when it rofe.

To God the Father in the height,
And to the Son, True Light of Light,
And Holy Ghoft all glory be,
Now and through all eternity.   Amen.

LIGHT IN THE DARKNESS.

A CHRISTMAS CAROL.

THE blaſts of chill December found
    The farewell of the Year,
And Night's ſwift ſhadows gathering
    round
O'ercloud the ſoul with fear;
But reſt you well, good Chriſtian men,
    Nor be of heart forlorn:
December's darkneſs brings again
    The light of Chriſtmas morn.

The welcome ſnow at Chriſtmas-tyde
    Falls ſhining from the ſkies:
On village paths and uplands wide
    All holy-white it lies;

It crowns with pearl the oaks and pines,
　　And glitters on the thorn ;
But purer is the Light that ſhines
　　On gladſome Chriſtmas morn.

At Chriſtmas-tyde the gracious moon
　　Keeps vigil while we ſleep,
And ſheds abroad her light's ſweet boon
　　On vale and mountain-ſteep :
O'er all the ſlumbering land deſcends
　　Her radiancy unſhorn ;
But brighter is the Light, good friends,
　　That ſhines on Chriſtmas morn.

'Twas when the World was waxing old,
　　And Night on Bethlehem lay,
The Shepherds ſaw the heavens unfold
　　A light beyond the day ;

Such glory ne'er had vifited
 A World with fin outworn ;
But yet more glorious light is fhed,
 On happy Chriftmas morn.

Thofe fhepherds poor, how bleft were they
 The angels' fong to hear !
In manger cradle as He lay,
 To greet their Lord fo dear !
The Lord of Heaven's Eternal height
 For us a Child was born ;
And He, the very Light of Light,
 Shone forth that Chriftmas morn !

Before His infant fmile afar,
 Were driven the hofts of hell ;
And ftill in fouls that childlike are
 His guardian love fhall dwell :

Light in the Darkneſs.

O then rejoice, good Chriſtian men,
Nor be of heart forlorn ;
December's darkneſs brings again
The Light of Chriſtmas morn.

NORVAL CLYNE.

FOR A YOUNG GIRL WITH A
BOOK OF CAROLS.

CAROL while yet thy life is in its spring,
  For spring-tide is the time for carolling :
  Sing while the dews are fresh, the day is
      young ;
Sweet songs found sweetest in the morning sung,
Ere yet the summer-noon, the winter-night
Harden the heart-springs, and the song-flowers
      blight ;
And airs of youth and Carols " light as air "
Seem but the echoes of the things that were.
      Up ! the sons of God are singing
          To the children of the plain ;
      Up ! the bells of Earth are ringing
          Back to Heaven their glad refrain :
      Up ! the day-star forth is flinging
      Lines of golden light, and stringing

Beads of dew thereon, to deck
With Love's necklace Morning's neck:
Up! then, and on Muſic's ſtring
Thread the pearls of ſong, and ſing—
In a lone bower far away
There is born a Babe to-day!

WILLIAM JOHN BLEW.

REST.

"There remaineth, therefore, a rest for the people of God."

 TOILERS in Life's vineyard,
    Who figh for perfect Reft,
    Whofe dim eyes, peering upward,
  With weight of years oppreffed,
Look for the blifsful flumber
  God gives to His beloved ;
Wait till the day is over,
  And He the tafk has moved.

Here, where the long long morning
  Melts into bufy noon,
The hours are all unreftful,
  But Evening cometh foon :

Lo on the lofty mountain
   The firſt faint ſhadow lies,
And God will draw His curtains
   Over the far-off ſkies.

Short ſlumbers has the pilgrim,
   His ready ſtaff in hand,
The ſoldier may but linger
   Till the foe is in the land :
The child muſt haſten homeward
   O'er hill and field and dell ;
And the golden gates are open
   Where they each in reſt ſhall dwell.

O weary heart, take courage !
   O feet, march on awhile !
O buſy hands, ſtill labour !
   Tired eyes ſhall ſee Him ſmile

Who has within His keeping,
  Still waiting for your claim,
The perfect Reſt of Heaven—
  The gladneſs of His Name.

No ſtorm diſturbs the waters,
  No wind ſhakes that repoſe ;
No trumpet calls to battle,
  Nor triumph then the foes :
Though ſeaſon follows ſeaſon,
  And year fades into year,
That reſt is ſtill remaining—
  That Heaven ſhall ſtill appear.

Take up the burden, Chriſtian,
  Bear thou, and labour on,
A little ſorrow only
  And the kingdom ſhall be won :

Only a few more footſteps,
   And then the tranquil Reſt;
Only a few more longings,
   And then the ſheltering Breaſt.

ALL SAINTS' AND ALL SOULS' DAYS
AT ALL SAINTS', LAMBETH, 1877.

MUSING over friends departed, loved ones
    known and miſſed and gone,
  As November's ſun was ſmiling ſpeaking
    ſummer to the morn,
Autumn-blooms were ſweet and odorous in their
  lateſt parting breath,—
Yet gazing upon Beauty I could only dream of
  Death.

Golden ſhower-clouds drifting purpled up between
    the Earth and ſky,
Seemed to pauſe, as though thanks giving, ere like
    tears they fell to die ;
Yet Earth in all its ſplendour was the goal where
  both were borne,

For I looked not fo far onward as the Refurrection-
    morn.

As All Saints' Night went gliding by, fhe wreathed
    the facred hours
With glory from her coronal of everlafting flowers:
There came, but not from Earth, a Voice that
    whifpered of the Bleft,
An echo from that far-off land in which the wan-
    derers reft.

The World had fobbed itfelf to fleep, all-filent after
    ftrife ;
The fhades of Death had vanifhed in the rays of
    endlefs Life ;
While that Voice Divine thrilled fweeter from the
    Home where angels foar,
As It whifpered " Saints are fhining as the ftars for
    evermore."

While the Holy Souls are thirſting for our Euchariſts
     and prayer—
Chriſt have pity ! Lady help them ! Mount they ſoon
     the golden ſtair !
And may all at laſt God's mercy know, when ſinking
     on Earth's breaſt,
" Where the wicked ceaſe from troubling and the
     weary are at reſt."

FREDERICK GEORGE LEE.

All Saints', Lambeth,
   Nov. 1, 1877.

M

AURORA.

I.

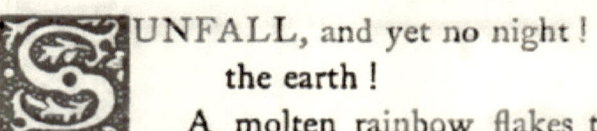

UNFALL, and yet no night ! Fire floods
the earth !
A molten rainbow flakes the northern
ſky !
The Polar gates uncloſe ; and gleaming forth
Troop the wild flames that glide and glare on high,
Tinged in their vaulted home with that deep
ruddy dye !

II.

Whence flaſh theſe myſtic ſignals ? what the ſcene
Where the red rivers find their founts of flame ?
Far, far away, where icy bulwarks lean

Along the deep, in feas without a name :
Where the vaft porch of Hades rears its giant
    frame !

III.

The underworld of fouls ! fever'd in twain :
    One, the fell North, perplexed and thick with
        gloom ;
And one, the South, that calm and glad domain,
    Where afphodel and lotus lightly bloom
    'Neath God's own Starry Crofs, the fhield of
        peaceful doom.

IV.

No queft of man fhall touch—no daring keel
    Cleave the dark waters to their awful bourne :
None fhall the living fepulchre reveal
    Where feparate fouls muft throng, and paufe ;
        and yearn
    For their far duft, the fignal, and their glad return.

v.

Ay ! ever and anon the gates roll wide,
   When whole battalions yield their fudden breath ;
And ghofts in armies gather as they glide,
   Still fierce and vengeful, from the field of death :
   Lo ! lightnings lead their hofts, and meteors glare
       beneath.

.   ROBERT S. HAWKER.

Morwenftow,
November 10, 1870.

MY HOME.

MAY all good angels watch around my
  dwelling,
    May holy ſpirits ſhield it with their care,
Each wayward thought within its precinɛts quelling:
    I aſk a bleſſing on it, in my prayer,
    From Thee, O Lord, Who ruleſt everywhere.

Angel of ſleep, O may'ſt thou ever carry
    Unto its inmates viſions fair and bright!
Angels of Peace and Love, within it tarry
    And ſhed around this hearth thy radiant light:
    Angel of Strength, defend it through the night.

Angel of Hope, when we are lone and dreary,
    Whiſper that dawn will follow midnight ſhade;
Angel of Faith, when our ſad hearts are weary,
    Uplift thy regal banner undiſmayed
    Before pale phantoms which make us afraid.

My Home.

Home, whence I truſt to paſs to life immortal
    When the calm ſleep of Death hath cloſed mine
        eyes ;
I look upon thee only as the portal
    Of God's bright Manſion far beyond the ſkies—
    Of the reſplendent Home in Paradiſe !

HELEN MONTAGU STUART.

ALPHABETICAL LIST OF AUTHORS.

INDEX OF FIRST LINES.

CHISWICK PRESS :—C. WHITTINGHAM, TOOKS COURT, CHANCERY LANE.

CATALOGUE

OF

RECENT PUBLICATIONS

ALDI

DISCIP

ANGL

PICKERING AND CO., LONDON

1883

CATALOGUE

OF

RECENT PUBLICATIONS.

ADDIS, JOHN. Elizabethan Echoes : or Poems, Songs, and Sonnets. Edited by his Sister. Fcap. 8vo. 3s. 6d.

"Mr. Addis's verses are no mere echoes; to their grace of form, and to the refinement of thought which informs them throughout, are added the higher charms of genuine idealism, pathetic intensity, and true human sympathy."—*Scotsman.*

ALTAR SERVERS' CEREMONIAL, the Order of Holy Communion, with Private Prayers for Servers, &c. 18mo. 9d.

ARUNDEL, LORD. The Scientific Value of Tradition : a correspondence between Lord Arundel of Wardour and Mr. E. Ryley. Crown 8vo. 5s.

AUGUSTINE, ST. MANUAL, or Little Book of the Contemplation of Christ. Square 12mo. *A facsimile reprint of the edition of* 1577, *with woodcut borders*, 2s. 6d.

"The antiquarian, and all who prize the works of the Fathers as aids to devotion, will welcome its publication."— *Christian World.*

"A faithful and admirably executed reproduction."— *Scotsman.*

"Many will be glad to possess this book in so interesting a form."—*Manchester Guardian.*

BADDELEY, W. ST. CLAIR. The Daughter of Jepthah, a Lyrical Tragedy, and other Poems. Fcap. 8vo. 5s.

BANQUET OF WIT, being a Varied Selection of Anecdotes, Bon Mots, &c., compiled from numerous sources by James Gray and J. J. B. Maidment. 12mo. 5s.

"The compilers have gone to many sources and have found many good things."—*Scotsman.*

BLAKE, WILLIAM. Poems : comprising Songs of Innocence and of Experience, together with Poetical Sketches and some Copyright Poems not in any other edition. 12mo. 2s. 6d.

"The songs only require to be known to be loved with a tenderness and enthusiasm which it is not given to many poets to arouse."—*Saturday Review.*

"The admirers of W. Blake as a poet—and they are rapidly increasing in number—owe much to Mr. Pickering for this reprint."—*Notes and Queries.*

BURIAL SERVICE. The Order for the Burial of the Dead. 16mo., *reprinted in red and black from the Sealed Copy of the Book of Common Prayer. In limp cloth, for the use of "Mourners,"* £2 10s. per hundred (6d. each).

*** This little book can be made to answer the purpose of a memorial card, by having the name of the departed person printed on the back of the title.

BURKE, U. R. Spanish Salt : a Collection of all the Proverbs which are to be found in "Don Quixote," with a literal English Translation, Notes, and Introduction. By ULICK RALPH BURKE. 12mo. cloth, 3s. 6d.

"We cordially recommend this little daintily-printed volume to those who care to con in a concentrated form those wise saws which, in connection with Squire Sancho, the shield-bearer of the immortal Don, have made him and his master immortal."—*Athenæum.*

"We are glad of all labours which make us read again the 'Don Quixote,' and increase our knowledge of its wealth of goodness and good humour, which bring out the excellences of that incomparable book, and the indomitable energy and noble bearing of its great and wise and courageous author ; therefore we thank Mr. Burke for what he has done," &c.—*Examiner.*

CALCOEN, CALICUT. Facsimile of a Dutch Narrative of the Second Voyage of Vasco da Gama to Calicut. Printed at Antwerp, *circa* 1504. With Introduction and Translation. By J. Ph. Berjeau. Small 4to. 5s.

CASWALL, E., of the Oratory, Birmingham. Poems and Hymns, original and translated. 12mo. 5s.

CEREMONIAL, NOTES ON. The Order of Holy Communion, with Prayers and Rubrics, from the Sarum Missal, for Use at the Altar, and Ritual Directions for Choral and Plain Celebrations of the Holy Eucharist, Solemn Evensong, and Funerals. *Second Edition, revised and enlarged, with illustrations and music.* Royal 8vo. 15s.

"We welcome the appearance of this carefully and well-printed volume as an interesting literary contribution to that which some people style liturgiology."—*Saturday Review.*

"Of the book itself, whatever may be thought of the elaborate details of ceremonial to which it descends, we must acknowledge that it has been compiled with a reverent care and a pious painstaking which evidently spring from the conviction, that nothing—not even what might be thought the most trifling detail—is unimportant which concerns the worship of God."—*John Bull.*

"Praise must be given to the diligence and learning displayed in the volume."—*Literary Churchman.*

CEREMONIAL GUIDE TO LOW MASS: or, Plain Directions for the Consecration and Administration of the Sacrament of the Holy Communion, adapted to the Use of the Church of England, by Two Clergymen. 12mo. 4s. 6d.

CHAMBERS, J. D. The Principles of Divine Worship. The Book of Common Prayer, illustrated by references to the Sarum Rites and Ceremonies, with numerous illustrations. *New Edition, revised, with additions.* 4to. £1 1s.

"This volume, of which the present is a new and enlarged edition, is a contribution as opportune as it is valuable to the ecclesiastical literature of our time."—*Saturday Review.*

—— Companion to the Holy Communion, with a Prefatory Office for Confession, translated and arranged from the Ancient English Offices. *Fifth Edition.* 18mo. 2s.

CHURCH CATECHISM, from the Book of Common Prayer, with Pictures and Explanations. *With 42 woodcuts.* 18mo. 1s. 3d., or 11s. 6d. per dozen.

CHURCH SERVICE, The Adult's, being the Liturgy according to the Use of the Church of England, for Use in Church; with Homely Explanations, Forms of Self-Examination, and Confession, &c. *With 22 woodcuts.* 18mo. 1s. 3d., or 11s. 6d. *per dozen.*

CHURCH SERVICE, The Child's, being the Liturgy according to the Use of the Church of England, for Use in Church; with Homely Explanations to be read at Home or at School. *With 22 woodcuts.* 18mo. 1s. 3d., or 11s. 6d. *per dozen.*

CHURTON, E. The Early English Church. *New Edition.* 12mo. maps and woodcuts, 4s.

"A convenient manual of the pre-Reformation history, by a scholar and divine of the old Anglican school. . . . . A fair and an interesting epitome of early English Church history."—*Contemporary Review.*

"Readable, interesting, and profitable from first to last. It may be consulted with advantage by students of all ages, and relied on as fair and impartial when more ambitious records fail to be so."—*Standard.*

COMPLIN, The Order of, according to the Use of the Illustrious Church of Sarum. Square 8vo. 2*s.*

COOK, KENINGALE. Love in a Mist, a Romantic Drama in Familiar Blank Verse. 12mo. 2*s.*

—— The Guitar Player, with Sundry Poems. 12mo. 3*s.*

—— The King of Kent, a Drama. 12mo. 2*s.*

—— Plays and Poems, viz., The King of Kent, The Guitar Player, Love in a Mist. 12mo. 7*s.* 6*d.*

DIVINE BREATHINGS: or, a Pious Soul thirsting after Christ, in a hundred pathetical Meditations. Edited by the Rev. W. J. LOFTIE. 18mo. 1*s.* 6*d.*

"A book of real merit as a serviceable manual of practical devotion."—*Saturday Review.*

"So many unimportant books have been reprinted in the last few years, that it is refreshing to welcome a little volume just published by Pickering and Co., 'Divine Breathings,' &c. . . . . . The 'Divine Breathings' are the work of a well-read and thoughtful man. . . . . . Taken as a whole they are, in a remarkable way, free from the slightest tinge of controversy, and may very profitably be read by either Catholic or Protestant. It would be unjust not to add that this little volume is an extremely pretty specimen of the Chiswick Press."—*Athenæum.*

"This is a book of devout piety and much learning, combined with a tender and beautiful style, which certainly reflects high honour upon the author, whoever he may have been."—*Christian World.*

DORE, J. R. Old Bibles; or, An Account of the Various Versions of the English Bible. Crown 8vo. 2*s.* 6*d.*

"Mr. Dore in the volume before us has endeavoured to give a plain, unvarnished account of the English Bible. . . . It is beautifully printed."—*Saturday Review.*

FANSHAWE, C. M. The Literary Remains of Catherine Maria Fanshawe, with Notes by the late Rev. Wm. Harness. Fcap. 8vo. *only* 250 *printed*, 3*s.*

"All Miss Fanshawe's playful and ladylike verses are well worth collection and preservation."—*Academy.*

FISHER, RICHARD TROTT. Works, uniformly printed. 4 vols. 8vo. £1 4*s.*

FRERE, J. H. The Works in Prose and Verse of the Right Honourable John Hookham Frere. Now first collected, with a Memoir by W. E. and Sir BARTLE FRERE. *Second Edition, with Additions.* 3 vols. crown 8vo. with two portraits engraved by C. H. Jeens, £1 4*s.*

—— *Large Paper,* 3 vols. 8vo. £2 2*s.*

"The compilers and editors of the present volumes have done good service in collecting the scattered writings of their distinguished uncle. As for the memoir by which these writings are prefaced, we cannot compliment them too highly upon its taste, or congratulate them too warmly on its interest. The pages will command the attention of all readers, the admiration of most ; and the entire production is, on every ground, one of the most valuable accessions to English literature."—*Standard.*

FULLER, MORRIS, M.A. Our Established Church : its History, Philosophy, Advantages, and Claims. Crown 8vo. 10*s.* 6*d.*

"In the interesting work bearing the title 'Our Established Church : its History, Philosophy, Advantages, and Claims,' the Rev. Morris Fuller gives us even more than its title promises, for he has added a chapter on the Anglican ordinal. Its main object is to point out the advantages of maintaining the Established Church in England, and this subject is treated with great vigour and much learning."—*Contemporary Review.*

—— A Voice in the Wilderness ; being Sermons preached at Dartmoor. Crown 8vo. 7*s.* 6*d.*

FULLER, T. David's Hainous Sinne, Heartie Repentance, Heavie Punishment. Crown 8vo. 7*s.* 6*d.*

. A facsimile reprint on hand-made paper of the original edition, which is so scarce as to be seldom met with. Only 100 copies were reprinted.

—— Life, with Notices of his Books, his Kinsmen, and his Friends. By J. EGLINGTON BAILEY. Thick 8vo. *numerous illustrations,* £1 5*s.*

GOLDIE, A. R. The Localism of Art. Crown 8vo. 2*s.* 6*d.*

HOME, F. WYVILLE. Songs of a Wayfarer. Crown 8vo. 7*s.* 6*d.*

"Rarely indeed, while wading through the volumes of

verse which crowd his table, does the reviewer come upon a
volume containing so much that is worthy of his attention as
is contained in 'Songs of a Wayfarer.' Mr. Home is a
true poet. . . . The workmanship is always artistic, an air
of culture hangs over all, and there is some genuine inspira-
tion. . . . . . We give Mr. Home such praise as we have
not oftentimes the pleasure of being able to accord."—
Athenæum.

" His perception in the nicest shades of word-painting is
thoroughly artistic ; his mastery of rhythm and metre is considerable ; and he seems to be endowed with a keen appreciation of the beautiful in nature and in art."—*Scotsman.*

JONES, EBENEZER. Studies of Sensation and Event.
12mo. 10s. 6d.

KARSLAKE, W. H. The Liturgy of the English Church
considered in its History, its Plan, and the Manner in which
it is intended to be used. 8vo. 8s. 6d.

KEBLE, J. The Christian Year : Thoughts in Verse for the
Sundays and Holy Days throughout the Year. 8vo. *beautifully printed,* 9s.

KEN, BISHOP. Christian Year ; or, Hymns and Poems
for the Holy Days and Festivals of the Church. 12mo. 6s.

LAMB, CHARLES AND MARY. Poetry for Children.
Edited and Prefaced by R. H. SHEPHERD. 12mo. *with woodcut initials, head and tail-pieces, a pretty little volume,* 3s. 6d.

LENDRUM, REV. A. The Reformation and Deformation,
their Principles and Results as affecting Doctrine, Worship,
and Discipline, a Letter to the Archbishop of Canterbury.
Thick 8vo. 15s.

—— The Judicial Committee, the Misgovernment of the Church,
and the Remedy. 8vo. *sewed,* 3s.

LONGFELLOW, H. W. Early Poems. Now first collected and edited by R. H. SHEPHERD. 12mo. 3s.

" Seldom, if ever, have verses fuller of rich promise or of
actual fulfilment been composed by a boy of seventeen."—
Examiner.

LUSCOMBE, A. M. Hymns translated into Rhyming Latin
Verse. Square crown 8vo. 3s. 6d.

" They are full of promise, being turned very happily
here and there."—*Church Times.*

"He has shown skill, refined taste, and vigour in his renderings, and considerable insight into the principles and structure of mediæval verse."—*Literary Churchman.*

LYRICS OF LIGHT AND LIFE. Fifty-four Original Poems. By CARDINAL NEWMAN, ALEXANDER LORD BISHOP OF DERRY, MISS CHRISTIANA G. ROSSETTI, Rev. GERARD MOULTRIE, Rev. J. S. B. MONSELL, Rev. W. J. BLEW, **AUBREY** DE VERE, Rev. H. N. OXENHAM, Rev. ED. CASWALL, &c. &c. Edited by Dr. F. G. LEE. *Second Edition, revised and enlarged. Handsomely printed with head and tail-pieces*, fcap. 8vo. 6s.

—— *Large Paper.* Crown 8vo. *printed on hand-made paper, only* 24 *so printed*, £1 1s.

"That quaint collection of **verse** which reflects the ascetic and ecstatic moods in the reaction of modern religious thought towards mediævalism. The poetic quality in **some** of these lyrics is indubitably good. . . . . . The antique typography and scroll borders of the volume are in keeping with the sentiment of the verses."—*Scotsman.*

MACLAGAN, T. J. Rheumatism, its Nature, its Pathology, and its Successful Treatment. 8vo. *with diagrams*, 10s. 6d.

"**The** chapters devoted **to** treatment **are ably** written. They commence with **a fairly exhaustive review** of all the methods **of** treatment which have **from time to** time been vaunted; and then the author passes **on to relate his** own introduction **and use** of salicin."—*Lancet.*

"It is **not a book** which **has** been rushed through the press, and **may be** lightly skimmed by the reader, for it contains **much solid** material."—*Medical Times and Gazette.*

"We can recommend this book **as well** worthy of a careful perusal, both in its theoretical **and** practical sections."—*Glasgow Medical Journal.*

"Must be regarded **as** a highly valuable contribution to medical literature, and it will unquestionably give important aid in advancing our knowledge on the subject of which he treats."—*Morning Post.*

"**A** valuable contribution to the literature of rheumatism, and will **have a lasting value.**"—*Birmingham Medical Review.*

"This work, by Dr. Maclagan, who was the first to introduce salicylic acid as a remedy for acute rheumatism, is full of suggestive remarks and valuable practical hints."—*Journal of Psychological Medicine.*

"From Dr. Maclagan's standpoint the subject is treated with a masterly hand, almost the whole literature of rheumatism being laid under contribution to furnish material in favour of his views."—*Monthly Homœopathic Review.*

"This work, in which the author develops his views, is written with admirable lucidity, and indicates clearly that he deals with his cases in a scientific spirit, and is an acute and thoughtful observer."—*Scotsman.*

MANCHESTER AL MONDO; a Contemplation of Death and Immortality. By HENRY MOUNTAGU, Earl of Manchester. Edited, with a Preface, by J. E. BAILEY, Author of the "Life of Fuller." 18mo. (uniform with "Divine Breathings"), 2*s.* 6*d.*

"The little book well deserves the honour conferred upon it by this elegant reprint, and the accompanying interesting introduction by Mr. J. E. Bailey."—*Daily News.*

"An interesting sketch of the author's career is furnished by Mr. J. E. Bailey by way of introduction to the present edition, and the exquisite appearance of the volume cannot fail to commend it to the reading public, apart from its intrinsic merits, which are of a high order."—*Rock.*

"'Manchester al Mondo' was quite worthy of republication for its own sake, and collectors will value it all the more for the elegance of its binding and the beauty of the printing."—*Manchester Examiner.*

"Mr. Bailey, of Manchester, has prefaced the little volume with a very interesting introduction, and the edition is in every way quaint and delightful."—*Liverpool Daily Post.*

"A dainty little reprint. . . . . Within and without it is a book for book lovers."—*Liverpool Albion.*

MANUEL, PRINCE DON JUAN, the Spanish Boccaccio. Count Lucanor, or the Fifty Pleasant Stories of Patronio, written by the Prince Don Juan Manuel, A.D. 1335-47, and now first translated from the Spanish into English, by JAMES YORK, M.D. 12mo, 6*s.*

"This curious collection of 'Pleasant Stories,' written a century before the invention of printing, has already been translated into French and German, and was well worth putting into an English dress. . . . . The notes, explanatory or illustrative of the stories are, as notes should be, brief, instructive, and to the point."—*Saturday Review.*

MEDITATIONS IN THE TEA ROOM, by M.P. *Second Edition*, fcap. 8vo. 5s.

> " Here we have a collection of thoughts, aphorisms, comments on men and things, showing a shrewd, somewhat cynical spirit, often expressed with much vigour and point."—*Spectator.*

MISSAL, THE MANUSCRIPT IRISH, belonging to the President and Fellows of Corpus Christi College, Oxford. Edited, with Introduction and Notes, by F. E. WARREN. 8vo. 5 *facsimiles*, 15s.

> " Mr. Warren has spared no trouble in his desire to give a sufficient edition of this important missal."—*Athenæum.*
>
> " The thanks of those interested in liturgical studies are due to the editor for the spirited manner in which he undertook, and has carried out, the work."—*Dublin Review.*
>
> " It does great credit to the diligence and care of Mr. Warren."—*Tablet.*

NEWMAN, CARDINAL. The Arians of the Fourth Century. Crown 8vo. 6s.

—— An Essay on the Development of Christian Doctrine. *New Edition, revised by the author.* Crown 8vo. 6s. ·

—— Certain Difficulties felt by Anglicans in Catholic Teaching Considered, in a Letter addressed to the Rev. E. B. Pusey, D.D., on occasion of his Eirenicon of 1864 ; and in a Letter addressed to the Duke of Norfolk on occasion of Mr. Gladstone's Expostulations of 1874.   Crown 8vo. 5s. 6d.

—— Discussions.   Crown 8vo. 6s.

Containing : I.—The celebrated "Letters of Catholicus" on Education (The Tamworth Reading Room). II.—An Internal Argument for Christianity. III.—On English Jealousy of "The Army" and "The Church." IV.—On the Relation between Scripture and the Catholic Creed, &c.

—— Miscellaneous and Critical Essays, comprising Articles on Poetical, Historical, and Biographical Subjects, written 1829-71.   2 vols. crown 8vo. 12s.

·   I.—The Nature of Poetry. II.—Rationalism. III.—Fall of De la Mennais. IV.—Palmer's View of the Church. V.—Epistles of Saint Ignatius. VI.—Anglican Prospects. VII.—The Anglo-American Church. VIII.—The Countess of Huntingdon. IX.—Catholicity of Anglican Church. X.—Antichrist. XI.—Milman's View of Christianity. XII.—The Reformation of the Eleventh

Century. XIII.—Private Judgment. **XIV.**—John Davi-
son. XV.—John Keble.

——Historical Sketches. Vol. I. crown 8vo. 6s.
   Containing : I.—The History of the Turks in their rela-
tion to Europe. II.—Life of Apollonius of Tyana. III.—
The Personal and Literary Character of Cicero. IV.—Of
Primitive Christianity.

—— Historical Sketches. **Vol. II.** crown 8vo. 6s.
   Containing : I.—A Sketch of the Life of Theodoret (now
first printed). II.—A Sketch of the Life of St. Chrysostom.
III.—Of the Mission of St. Benedict. IV.—Of the Bene-
dictine Schools. V.—The Church of the Fathers, containing Sketches of St. Basil, St. Gregory, St. Anthony, St.
Augustine, Demetrius, and St. Martin.

—— Historical Sketches. **Vol. III.** crown 8vo. 6s.
   Containing : I.—A Sketch of the Rise and Progress of
Universities. II.—An Essay on the Northmen and Nor-
mans in England and Ireland. III.—A Review of Mediæval
Oxford. IV.—An Historical Sketch of the Convocation of
Canterbury.

—— On Miracles. Two Essays on Scripture Miracles, and on
Ecclesiastical. Crown 8vo. 6s.

—— Tracts, Theological and Ecclesiastical. Crown 8vo. 8s.
   Containing : I.—Dissertatiunculæ. II.—The Doctrinal
Causes of Arianism. III.—Apollonarianism. IV.—St.
Cyril's Formula. V.—Ordo de Tempore. VI.—On the
various revisions of the Douay Versions of Scripture.
   Several of the above have NEVER BEEN PREVIOUSLY
PRINTED, others are from periodicals now inaccessible.

—— The Via Media of the Anglican Church. Vol. I. containing the whole of the "Lectures on the Prophetical Office of
the Church Viewed Relatively to Romanism and Popular
Protestantism," as published in 1837; with New Preface
and Notes. Vol. II. containing Occasional Letters and
Tracts written between 1830 and 1841. **2** vols. crown 8vo.
6s. each.

—— Idea of a University, Considered in Nine Discourses, Occasional Lectures, and Essays. Crown 8vo. 7s.

—— Select Treatises of St. Athanasius in Controversy with the
Arians. Freely Translated. **2** vols. crown 8vo. 15s.

PALMER, W. Compendious Ecclesiastical History. *New
   Edition.* Fcap. 8vo. 4s.

PAYNE, JOHN. The Masque of Shadows, and Other Poems. Fcap. 8vo. 7s.

—— Intaglios, Sonnets. 12mo. 3s. 6d.

"Excellent scholar's work in poetry."—*Academy.*

—— Lautrec, a Poem. 12mo. 3s. 6d.

"His command of melodious language and imaginative power are undoubted ; and his place among poets of that new school of which Mr. Rossetti is the prophet, is a high one."—*John Bull.*

SANDYS, R. H. In the Beginning: Remarks on Certain Modern Views of the Creation. *Second Edition.* Crown 8vo. 6s.

"Abounding . . . in passages of deep thought, religious feeling, and manly eloquence."—*Times.*

"The author assails mercilessly the various schools of modern thought, as they delight to call themselves. . . . The veils are drawn from their sophistries, and their theories are keenly dissected ; while the writer's own conclusions are beautifully drawn out."—*Tablet.*

—— Antitheism ; Remarks on its Modern Spirit. Crown 8vo. 4s. 6d.

SCOTT, P. Christianity and a Personal Devil. *Second Edition.* Fcap. 8vo. 5s.

SHIRLEY, E. P. A History of the County of Monaghan. Folio, with numerous Illustrations, Antiquarian and Heraldic, *only 250 copies printed,* £4 4s.

"This work bids fair to stand at the head of all Irish histories devoted to similar local, social, and family illustrations."—*Notes and Queries.*

"Mr. Shirley's history is gleaned from many and varied sources, the reference to the authorities being always given. Its great value consists in the care with which whatever of interest was anywhere accessible has been collected. The freshness of the pedigrees, and the accuracy of the inscriptions from sepulchral monuments, will render the book indispensable in all libraries."—*Academy.*

SONGS OF SOCIETY from Anne to Victoria. Edited. with Notes and an Introduction, by W. DAVENPORT ADAMS. Fcap. 8vo. 5s.

—— *Large Paper (only 25 printed),* £1 1s.

"A charming selection . . . selected with admirable

taste and true appreciation. A volume upon which all lovers of genuine poetry will place the highest value."— *Morning Advertiser.*

"An excellent little volume for a lady's drawing-room."— *Vanity Fair.*

"The selection is a good one. It makes a very pleasant volume, pretty sure, wherever one opens it, to yield something worth reading or renewing acquaintance with."— *Spectator.*

TENNYSONIANA. *Second Edition, revised and enlarged.* Fcap. 8vo. 6s.

—— *Large Paper (only 25 printed),* £1 1s.

"There is a great deal in the volume which must prove interesting to the admirers of the Laureate. . . . Altogether the work should be welcome as a book of reference."— *Graphic.*

"This book must be considered almost indispensable to any one who desires to have a thorough knowledge of Tennyson's writings."— *The Week.*

TRELAWNY, E. J. Records of Shelley, Byron, and the Author. *New Edition, greatly enlarged.* 2 vols. crown 8vo. with portraits and plates, 12s.

"His book stands alone in the voluminous and confused literature which deals with the lives of Shelley and Byron." —*Saturday Review.*

"We will only add that Trelawny's merits as a biographer consist mainly in clear insight, the power of saying exactly what he means in language that is at once plain, terse, and pointedly descriptive, without any amplifying or circumlocution, and a wholly unconventional tone and temper of mind. He observes well, remembers well, and expresses well."—*Academy.*

"As a biographic source for the last years of Shelley's life, Mr. Trelawny's book is invaluable. . . . Even if written by an outsider, this account of a poetic still-life would be attractive; but coming from one who for months was Shelley's constant companion, who performed his funeral rites, and broke the news of his death to his widow, it may fairly be said to rank with the standard works of biographic literature."—*Pall Mall Gazette.*

WACE, H. Christianity and Morality; being the Boyle Lectures for 1874-5. By HENRY WACE, D.D., Prebendary of St. Paul's, Preacher of Lincoln's Inn, Professor of Ecclesiastical History, King's College, London, Bampton Lecturer for 1879 in the Univ. of Oxford, &c. *Sixth and Cheaper Edition.* 1878, crown 8vo. 6s.

"Mr. Wace's book is one of the very few of its kind which have in them not only intellectual, but also spiritual force."—*Spectator.*

"Mr. Wace seems to us to have made by far the most important and valuable contribution to English theological literature that has been made for many years."—*Congregationalist.*

—— The Foundations of Faith ; being the Bampton Lectures for the year 1879. *Second Edition.* 8vo. 7s. 6d.

"True and good and seasonable."—*Spectator.*

"To this work, as a whole, we give a cordial welcome."—*Church Quarterly Review.*

"Mr. Wace has done noble service in this suggestive volume."—*Evangelical Magazine.*

WALTONIANA. Inedited Remains in Verse and Prose of Izaak Walton, author of the "Complete Angler." With Notes and a Preface by R. H. SHEPHERD. Crown 8vo. 7s. 6d.

"This dainty little volume distinctly belongs to the class of literary luxuries, and not to the loaves and fishes of sturdy bibliomania. A hearty reader or a gluttonous collector will disdain its brevity and the miscellaneous character of its contents, but to the critic and literary historian it is not without interest and even value."—*Athenæum.*

"As this charming little volume, with its curiously old-fashioned typography, attests, Walton was for the best part of his life a writer of verses, if not a poet, and in all his verses the simplicity and serenity of his cheerful and affectionate nature shine out with a pleasant force."—*Daily News.*

WARBURTON, R. E. EGERTON-. Hunting Songs. *Sixth Edition.* 12mo. *with vignette title,* 5s.

—— Songs and Verses on Sporting Subjects. 12mo. 2s. 6d.

"All who remember—and who has forgotten it?—the 'Tantivy Trot' will eagerly take up 'Songs and Verses on Sporting Subjects,' by R. E. Egerton-Warburton (Pickering), and they will not be disappointed. There is much that deserves remembrance in the unpretending little book."—*Graphic.*

"'Songs and Verses on Sporting Subjects,' by R. E. Egerton-Warburton (Pickering), comprises another addition to the poetry of the chase by that admirable writer whose hunting songs of Cheshire and other counties have long earned him the title of the 'poet-laureate' of the hunting field."—*Sporting Gazette.*

—— Poems and Epigrams. Crown 8vo. *only* 250 *printed,* 7*s.* 6*d.*

—— Twenty-Two Sonnets. Small 4to. 11 *full-page illustrations,* 12*s.* 6*d.*

WARWICK, ARTHUR. Spare Minutes; or, Resolved Meditations and Premeditated Resolutions. Edited by the Rev. W. J. LOFTIE. 18mo. uniform with "Divine Breathings." 1*s.* 6*d.*

"This is a delightful little book, printed at the Chiswick Press, elegantly attired, rivalling the conciseness of its literary style in its typography and binding ; so that he who has not too many spare minutes may well carry these about with him in his waistcoat-pocket.—*St. James's Gazette.*

WILBERFORCE, R. T. The Five Empires ; an Outline of Ancient History. *Fifteenth Edition.* 12mo. maps and plates, 3*s.* 6*d.*

"When a book has reached its fifteenth edition it passes beyond the limits of criticism and can speak for itself. The work before us is well known, and of its usefulness there can be no question."—*Church and State.*

"It is unnecessary to make many comments on a volume which has been so widely successful as Mr. Wilberforce's 'Five Empires.'"—*Pall Mall Gazette.*

WINSCOM, CAVE. Tsoé, and other Poems. 12mo. 3*s.* 6*d.*

—— Waves and Caves, and other Poems. 12mo. 3*s.* 6*d.*

—— Camden, and other Poems. 12mo. 3*s.* 6*d.*

—— Wild Oats. Square 12mo. 2*s.* 6*d.*

YACHTSMAN'S HOLIDAYS, A; or, Cruising in the West Highlands. By the "GOVERNOR." *Second Edition.* Crown 8vo. cloth, with illustrations on wood, 5*s.*

"Although the 'Governor,' in his brief preface, modestly affects to apologize for the national absence of humour, in reality he shows a quick perception of comic sides of character ; and, as he can tell a capital story, he makes his narrative very amusing. He takes off the islanders and their broken Anglo-Saxon vernacular in a manner that would do credit to Mr. William Black. . . . . Altogether, the little volume is greatly to be recommended to any adventurer in those

Western waters ; and, thanks to its modest proportions, there can be no objection to shipping it among the sea-stores of even such a vessel as the ' Ilma.' "—*Saturday Review.*

" Anyone who intends cruising north during the coming summer would do well to obtain ' A Yachtsman's Holidays,' it contains so many valuable hints of the places most worth seeing, and many useful sailing directions obtained from personal experience. . . . . The volume is of a very handy size, and we think every yachtsman should find a place for it in his book locker."—*Field.*

" Four cruises are described, each in a separate craft. . . . Good seamanship was, of course, needed when cruising in such small boats among the northern lochs, but the 'Governor' evidently knows what he is about when the tiller is in his hand as well as he does when he takes up the pen. The result of both gifts is, that he not only escaped 'the dangers of the deep,' but that the public are indebted to him for a book whose only fault is its brevity."—*Globe.*

" He interests his readers in his craft, and in the voyagings he made by their help, giving us a very lively and graphic picture of life on, or rather, we should say, off the West Coast."—*Spectator.*

"The ' Governor ' is evidently one whose company is to be desired on a yachting cruise. He is a man of few dislikes and many sympathies. . . . . We are certain he will not want readers."—*Glasgow Herald.*

CHISWICK PRESS:—C. WHITTINGHAM AND CO. TOOKS COURT, CHANCERY LANE.

www.ingramcontent.com/pod-product-compliance
Lightning Source LLC
Chambersburg PA
CBHW030541040726
47497CB00008B/2545